Selbuvotter

Biography of a Knitting Tradition

Text, illustrations, and photos by Terri Shea
Cover design and layout assistance by Rosemary Hill
Proofreading by Karen Campbell
Printed by Snohomish Publishing Company

Spinningwheel LLC
P.O. Box 30863
Seattle, WA 98113

http://www.selbuvotter.com/

This book was produced on a Dell® Inspiron E1505 laptop, using the Adobe® Creative Suite® family of products: Adobe Photoshop® CS2 for photographs, Adobe Illustrator® CS2 for charts, and Adobe InDesign® CS2 for layout. The book face is Adobe Garamond Pro, OpenType® version. Titles are Adobe Jenson Pro OpenType. The sans serif font used in captions is Myriad Pro OpenType. Photographs were taken using a Canon Powershot A700.

Every effort has been made to ensure that all the information in this book is accurate. However, due to differing conditions, differences in gauge, needles, yarns, and individual skills, the publisher cannot be responsible for any injuries, losses, or other damages that may result from the use of the information in this book.

Printed in the United States of America

10 9 8 7 6 5 4 3

ISBN: 978-0-9793126-0-1

Selbuvotter
Biography of a Knitting Tradition

by Terri Shea

Spinningwheel LLC
Seattle, Washington

Foreword

Sitting in an electrically-lit room, with a modern furnace and a pattern downloaded from who-knows-where-across-the-world, it's easy for a twenty-first century knitter to fall into nostalgia about the early days of knitting.

We close our eyes and imagine the scene. An old woman sits in a rocking chair next to a crackling fire, a lace shawl around her shoulders and a blanket on her lap. Near her feet sits an old dog and a basket overflowing with yarns of all colors. The old man sits opposite with a book or a pipe or a bit of whittling. They rock together silently, and the old woman knits on a bit of fine work, a lacy shawl or patterned sock. A storm rages outside, but here in the cozy farm cottage all is warm and well.

Or we picture the opposite, a family so wracked by poverty that father works to the bone just to pay the rent and poor mother must slave every spare minute over her needles to put food on the family table. Her gaunt, pale children (too many of them) hold the skeins between their twiglike hands while she winds the yarn into balls, then she feeds the children a thin gruel and sends them to shiver under threadbare blankets, while she knits by firelight long into the dark night.

I have no doubt that both scenarios played true in places, at different times. Comfortable people often enjoyed knitting for its own sake. And there are more than enough written reports from knitters in Shetland whose situation was dire indeed. Knitting has been a cottage industry in many areas of Europe, bringing in extra money in times of difficulty.

But I hope to get beyond stereotypes and paint a broader picture of the life of one particular tradition of knitting, a picture that includes the gentle old women but also determined businessmen, dedicated historians, and mostly thousands of craftswomen - and men - who knitted for the love of the work itself as well as the extra money it could provide.

I came to this project serendipitously. I enrolled in a Museum Studies program through the University of Washington in 2005, looking for a new career direction after motherhood and job market research made returning to my career as a web developer less than appealing. In the course of my studies I worked as an intern at The Nordic Heritage Museum (NHM) in Seattle. NHM collects and preserves the history of the settlers who came to the Pacific Northwest from the five Nordic countries: Norway, Sweden, Denmark, Finland, and Iceland. The collection is extensive for a small museum, and naturally contains a large number of textiles.

When the Collections Manager, Lisa Hill-Festa, learned of my background as a knitter, she decided to put me to work on the catalog, adding additional data to the records for the museum's collection of mittens.

Only another knitter can imagine the thrill of excitement I felt when I first opened the grey archival box, folded back the acid-free tissue, and saw pair after pair after pair of beautiful, well made, and gorgeously patterned mittens. The urge to slip my hand into that soft wool was overpowering, and I had to put my hands behind my back to keep from doing it. As the cliché goes, I drank them in with my eyes alone.

Three mornings a week I came in for a few hours, measured the width, length, and gauge, described the pattern, and checked the paper records for clues about these masterpieces. Museum Days became a sacred time for me, to regain my space as a person and not just as mother and wife, and to connect with the knitters who had created these beautiful pieces, seemingly for me alone to view and enjoy.

As NHM is a small museum with limited staffing, the mitten collection had not been categorically reviewed by someone with the expertise of a knitter, so this was a tremendous opportunity for me. As I studied each pair in depth I began to see similarities that a non-knitter wouldn't notice: how the palm patterns on several were identical, or how the cuff of one pair was the same as the thumb on another. I had been primarily a texture knitter, but looking at all the stranded patterns made me long to try it out myself.

One morning I was waxing poetically over a particularly lovely pair with a feminine, lacy cuff and I commented to Lisa how much I'd love to chart and duplicate them. "That would make a wonderful practicum project for you!" Lisa exclaimed. Within a few days she had received permission from the museum director and the UW coordinator, and I had myself a final project: to document the mittens.

Sounds simple enough, doesn't it?

In the course of my charting and research I recognized that more than half the collection were the Selbu type mittens; a Norwegian style characterized by a white background and black pattern, typically a variation on the eight-pointed star. After I finished the cataloging I decided to focus my research on Selbu mittens for simplicity's sake, since the collection had mittens from so many different regions.

Not more than a week after I had charted the last pair of Selbu mittens my home was burglarized. My laptop computer - with all of my charts - was stolen. I had been planning to back everything up but "never got around to it." With no data and a deadline approaching I knew I would have to start over from scratch and rechart every pair.

Let this be a lesson to you: Back up your data, early and often.

I found, once again, that every cloud does indeed have a silver lining, because one evening when I was pouting about having to rebuild my charts I did some web surfing to see what I could find. I suppose it was work avoidance more than anything else. I looked at Norwegian yarn company sites, trolled through search engines, read a lot of blogs, and somehow, through links, I found myself at the website of the Selbu Bygdemuseum, the folk museum in Selbu, the village where the mittens were born. (The URL is in the bibliography.) I'd been searching for historical information to round out what I had learned from studying the mittens themselves, but little has been published in English. Finally, here was the jackpot. A quick e-mail to the museum, another search for a Norwegian-to-English translation program, and I was inspired all over again.

A few weeks later I was knitting in a yarn store, when a local yarn rep, Sandy Blue, came in. I had met her before but hadn't seen her in sometime, so we chatted and caught up while the store owner decided which yarns to order for fall. I was working on a pair of mittens and told Sandy the story of my project. She recommended I contact Annemor Sundbø ("She's really nice!"). So I sent Annemor an e-mail, and of course, she *is* really nice, and she gave me permission to reproduce some of her favorite mittens and gloves, too. When the package came in the mail I fell in love all over again.

The book you are holding is the sum of my research, and, more importantly, the summary of a knitting tradition that begins with a young woman on a lonely hillside, and ends when you bind off your last mitten. It covers a range of about a hundred and fifty years, thousands of miles of space, tons of wool, and generations of knitters. It is a never ending yarn; a thread looped through time and space, and a tale with a certain beginning but no certain end.

There are two kinds of knitters: those who create traditions, and those who keep them.

My work is dedicated to them both.

Acknowledgments

The term "self published book" is an oxymoron. I am deeply indebted to my guide into the world of Norwegian knitting, Annemor Sundbø. Her research, published in *Everyday Knitting,* was instrumental to me in writing this book; her loan of some of her favorite mittens and gloves was invaluable. Every time I thought I had this story down pat she would email with new tidbits of information and I would be off on another hunt. I also thank Karen Campbell, a sweet friend whose very gentle encouragement gave me the impetus to begin this project. Karen also proofed the manuscript and prevented countless errors from going to press. To Lisa Hill-Festa, Kirsten Olsen, and Marianne Forssblat of the Nordic Heritage Museum where this project was conceived; and to Birgitta Odén, curator with the Trøndelag Folkemuseum. Arnhild Hillesland translated the Selbu Husflidscentral standards document. Thanks to Meg Swansen for the Jamieson & Smith and Satakieli yarn and especially the encouragement. Annichen (Lillen) Bøhn Kassel provided information and documents about her mother Annichen Sibbern Bøhn, for which I am grateful.

All of the knitters who helped make samples have my deep gratitude: Wendy Colbert, Angela Ho, Kim Myrhe, Michelle Molis, Karen Campbell, Holly Odegard, Elka Priest, Anne Hansen, Karen Walter, Denise Satterlund, Elisabeth Tostrup, Pat Martin, Mary Schmelzer, Anne Turner, Miriam Felton (twice), Ivete Tecedor, Kristin Eilertsen, Vanessa Grimmett, Eyja M. Brynjarsdóttir, and Judy Seip, in no particular order. Thanks, Rosemary Hill for your design advice. Nancy Bush, Beth Brown-Reinsel and Meg Swansen for reviewing the work. Also, thanks to the wonderful people at my favorite local yarn stores, The Weaving Works, The Fiber Gallery, and Village Yarn & Tea. Whenever my brain got too full I would rush to the closest yarn store and dump every thought about mittens and gloves and Selbu and post-feminism in the nineteenth century. I know I sounded like a crazy person, thanks for smiling and nodding. I can't forget my printer, Snohomish Publishing; they're terrific. Special thanks of course, to my family, who have been forced to live in Mittenlandia for more than a year. Brian's finally got his slippers, and I am so proud of Heather, who watched pair after pair of pretty mittens go in the box. Next pair's for you, sweetie. Promise. ❧

Alibris Packing Slip

Ordered by: Madolin Ross   **Ship to:**

Madolin Ross
314 Kerr Avenue
DENTON, MD 21629-1425
UNITED STATES

Visit MOUNTAIN LAUREL BOOKS at http://mtlaurel.alibrisstore.com again!

PN #	Item ID	Alibris ID	Media Type	Title / Author	Order Date
44376062-1	49032	B039197266	BOOK	Selbuvotter Biography of a Knitting Tradition Terri Shea	Dec, 12 2011

New 0979312604. New book. Black and white star patterned mittens of Norway. 30 patterns for Selbu mittens and gloves taken from two antique collections: The Nordic Heritage Museum in Seattle, and Annemor Sundbø, author of "Everyday Knitting" and "Setesdal

Alibris Return Information

Alibris guarantees the condition of every item as it is described on our Web site. If you are not satisfied that your item is as described, please visit the following page for **important return instructions**:

http://www.alibris.com/returns

All return requests must be submitted via the Alibris Web site. Any item returned without accompanying paperwork and/or more than 60 days after its shipment date will be discarded and you will not be eligible to receive a refund.

Problems? Questions? Suggestions? Send e-mail to Alibris Customer Service at info@alibris.com

Contents

History • 13

*The Mother of Selbu Knitting ... Bridal Finery ...
Early Trade ... Organization ... The Evangelist ...
The War Years and After*

Technique • 29

*Before you Begin ... Anatomy of a Mitten ...
Mutation: Gloves ... Making your Mittens your
Own*

The Patterns • 39

Over 30 Patterns Reconstructed from Antiques

Resources • 124

*Nordic Heritage Museum ... Everyday Knitting
... Bibliography ... Last but not Least*

History

The early history of knitting in general, and Scandinavian knitting specifically, has been well documented in other texts, especially *A History of Hand Knitting* by Richard Rutt and *Traditional Scandinavian Knitting* by Sheila McGregor. I don't intend to repeat this work, but I do want to place our topic in the context of Norwegian history and culture.

In a nutshell, nomads of the Arabian Peninsula probably invented knitting; the Moorish conquerors of Spain brought their skills to Europe. By the sixteenth century knitting technology had spread across Europe. Spain and England produced and exported fine knitted goods such as silk nightshirts, silk stockings, and gloves. Lower-class people knit everyday items for themselves. These were worked mostly in single color, with knit and purl patterns forming the decoration. (McGregor, *Traditional Scandinavian Knitting*, 12-13.)

Denmark ruled Norway since the Black Plague had killed nearly half of its population in the fourteenth century. During the Napoleonic Wars, Denmark-Norway claimed neutrality but had secretly traded with France and practiced guerilla warfare against Britain. They were caught and defeated in 1814 at the end of the Gunboat War. Britain placed trade embargoes on Denmark-Norway, and the import of luxury goods, including the fine silk knitwear from Spain and England, and replacements had to be reproduced at home using local materials.

Norway took its first steps toward independence

Selbu

later that year when it was ceded from Denmark to Sweden as a separate state ruled by Sweden's monarchy. Political independence gave the people new pride in their nationality. Newspaper articles advocated the use of locally produced goods as an act of patriotism, and in 1839 new laws were enacted that struck down the old guild systems and allowed women to legally sell knitted items produced from their own wool. (Sundbø, *Setesdal Sweaters,* 32-33.) Knitting took on a political and economic importance, like the role homespun and handmade goods played in the American Revolution, as described in *No Idle Hands* by Anne L. Macdonald. Local manufacture of goods to be used locally, from local materials, would provide independence from foreign nations; Norwegians meeting Norwegian needs. To firmly display Norway's emerging identity new designs would be required, with a special Norwegian style, and knitters across the country filled the need.

By the nineteenth century knitting was well established as a useful and portable craft all over Europe, and was practiced by both men and women. It was about this time that stranded knitting was blossoming across northern Europe, especially Scandinavia and Britain.

"The Mother of Selbu Knitting"

The district of Selbu is located an hour's drive east of Trondheim, in the

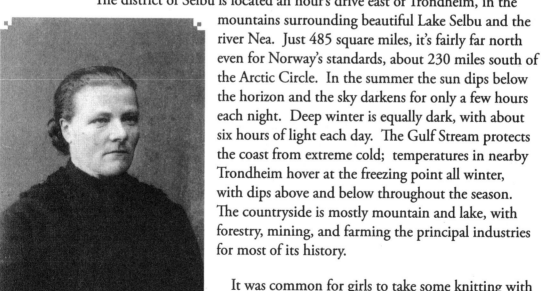

mountains surrounding beautiful Lake Selbu and the river Nea. Just 485 square miles, it's fairly far north even for Norway's standards, about 230 miles south of the Arctic Circle. In the summer the sun dips below the horizon and the sky darkens for only a few hours each night. Deep winter is equally dark, with about six hours of light each day. The Gulf Stream protects the coast from extreme cold; temperatures in nearby Trondheim hover at the freezing point all winter, with dips above and below throughout the season. The countryside is mostly mountain and lake, with forestry, mining, and farming the principal industries for most of its history.

Marit Guldseth Emstad. Photo Courtesy Selbu Bygdemuseum

It was common for girls to take some knitting with them into the hills and work while watching the herds during the long summer days. In the summer of 1856, Marit Guldseth worked for a farmer named Jo Kjøsnes. Another girl who worked at the farm had made him a pair of stockings with black stitches "snaking up the leg." Jo asked Marit if she could do the same. Looking at the determined expression in the photo of Marit, I can see her as a person who would take a tease and turn it into a dare.

Set with the challenge of knitting something entirely new, Marit tried alternating stitches of two different colors of yarn. She experimented and practiced all summer, trying different designs. Norway has centuries-old traditions in weaving and needlework, so Marit had studied textiles her whole life; the bridal embroideries and woven tapestries that had been created by her mother, grandmothers, aunts, cousins, and neighbors. She incorporated the eight-pointed rose designs she had seen since birth into her work. At the age of sixteen, Marit created mittens using the selburose, knit in white and patterned with natural black wool.

Marit and her sister wore the new mittens to church one Sunday. If her family had been less respected, the other women might have rejected her mittens as outlandish and we would never have heard of Selbu, Norway. Luckily for her, and for them, Marit's mittens were extremely popular, and one by one the girls and women of the district learned to knit in her new way. Each wanted to create a design even more beautiful than the others.

The story ends well for Marit. She is known in Norway as "The Mother of Selbu Knitting." A Trondheim newspaper published an article about her in 1927 and she was able to enjoy the recognition her invention deserved. Marit died in 1929.

It is an extraordinarily rare occurrence to be able to identify the exact place and time that a cultural advance is initiated. Who discovered fire? Who used the first wheel? Who wove the first twill? Who knit the first gansey? In **Aran Knitting**, Alice Starmore has stated her belief that the Aran sweater tradition was invented by a single knitter, but the identity of that inventor has been lost. Selbu may be unique in remembering the origin of their best knitting tradition. Marit (Guldseth) Emstad, born 1841, deserves recognition for her work. What started as a dare was to become a local tradition.

Bridal Finery

Marit's mittens were so popular that everyone wanted a pair. She and her sister taught their friends and neighbors how to knit in the new way. The white and black patterned mittens passed from an interesting single invention into the folk costume of the area, replacing the old nålbinding mittens worn previously. Selbu knitting became *the* knitting to wear for special occasions. Similar to the roles mittens played in nineteenth century Estonia, Selbu mittens were used as gifts and status symbols in marriage rituals.

Getting engaged and then married was no simple thing for a girl of Selbu. According to the tradition, a bride had to start knitting well before the wedding. First she had to make a special pair of selburose patterned stockings for the bridegroom; then she knit stockings for the father of the groom, the brothers and brothers-in-law, and the bridegroom's godchildren. The bridegroom's mother received a new dress, and his sisters and sisters-in-law received new blouses. All of these were handmade, of course, and all were the responsibility of the bride. If she couldn't or didn't want to sew the blouses and dresses herself, she could knit extra socks and mittens and trade them at the general store. (Selbu Bygdemuseum, Bush, *Folk Knitting in Estonia.*)

All of the men invited to the wedding would receive a new pair of mittens to take home with them as a gift, but these were not knit by the bride. They were knitted by the women who had been invited, and delivered to the bride a few days before the wedding. The bride would clean and decorate the bridal

loft, and hang the mittens carefully on a rope or rod where they would be on display throughout the wedding. She had to pay careful attention, because it was her responsibility to make sure that each man took home the mittens his wife had knitted. If Erling took home the mittens that Karl's wife had made, the bride would look like a fool. (Selbu Bygdemuseum.)

Pattern Annemor #3. From the collection of Annemor Sundbø.

These wedding traditions were developed and followed in the late nineteenth and early twentieth centuries, only dying out during World War II. (McGregor, *Traditional Scandinavian Knitting*, 46.) It is my belief that the patterns NHM #10 (pp110-112) and Annemor #3 (pp45-47) were knit for wedding gifts. Both pair are worked at a fine gauge, around 9 stitches per inch, which is typically seen in pre-war mittens. (Post-war mittens were often knit in DK wool at larger gauge, 6.5 or 7 stitches per inch.) The date 1932 is in the time frame that selbuvotter were knit for weddings, and the letters S O could be the groom's initials; the donor who gave the mittens to the museum donated them in honor of her father, whose last name was Strang. And perhaps Erling's wife worked his name into this pair, to make sure no mistakes were made when it was time to hand out the gifts.

Early Trade

The first general store in Selbu was opened by Fredrik Birch. Born in Trondheim in 1826, Birch moved to Selbu and started his business around 1860. A successful businessman, Birch's family would eventually run the store, a farm, a bakery, a post office, and a millstone mining operation on Kvenrfjellet Mountain, the largest millstone producer in Norway. (Selbusjøen Hotel & Gjestegård website.)

When Birch traveled to Kristiania (Oslo) in 1883 to attend an industrial exposition, he took some of the patterned mittens with him. The mittens were very popular; he saw a market and decided to meet it. (Selbu Bygdemuseum.) Birch and another businessman, Gustav Christophersen, began buying mittens from local knitters, or accepting them in trade for merchandise. They traded or sold the mittens to merchants in other areas; by the end of the 1890's mitten sales earned around four or five hundred kroner annually, at a profit of 1-2 kr per pair. (Selbu Bygdemuseum.)

With the turn of the century, the millstone industry took a downswing and hundreds of men were put out of work. Women were able to supplement or even replace the family income by selling their knitting. Knitted items, including mittens, gloves, hats, scarves, socks and stockings, could be sold or traded for supplies such as coffee, sugar, tobacco, or even larger items like shoes or other articles of clothes. With little cash money, a Norwegian family could grow their own vegetables and some meat, fish during the summer, and trade knitted goods for necessities that couldn't be made at home.

All around Norway at this same time, the Husflid organization was forming. Husflid, or the Norwegian Home Arts and Crafts organization, serves the dual purpose of supporting the traditional crafts by providing information and supplies, and providing a marketplace for artists to sell their work. Marit delivered the first pair of white and black star-patterned mittens to the Trondheim Husflid in 1897. (Sundbø, *Everyday Knitting*, 40.)

In a district with around 4,000 residents, the number of knitters was limited. Those who did knit, did so whenever an opportunity presented itself; folk tradition evolved into a large scale commercial endeavor. Some women even knit while walking between farms, basket over the forearm, or while shopping in the stores. Any spare moment could be used to earn a little money. The knitters loved most to gather together in a kaffeeklatsch, sharing light and company as they worked. A good knitter could make a pair of mittens in a single day. The spirit of competition held by as many as two thousand independent knitters created a huge wealth of designs, from their own imagination or from other textiles or designs. Selbu is on the road between Trondheim and Sweden, so this location would help spread their popularity as well as bring in new ideas for designs.

Some knitters in Norway today can identify from which farm a particular design originated, and patterns are named for the farm or family or situation where they were designed: *Emstadrosa* (Emstad rose), *Kallarstrørosa* (Kallarstø rose), *værhornrosa* (ram's horn rose), *kaffekånnet* (coffee can).

Eventually high demand and the limited number of knitters took a toll on the quality of knitting in Selbu and "selbu knitting" came to mean shoddy or poor quality work; much like "Made in China" was to the US consumers in the 1970's and 1980's. Mistakes were made in patterns, some knitters used too-large needles, others knit small mittens and blocked them larger to sell as adult sizes. Overall consistency was lacking. Caught between rising demand and deteriorating quality, the Selbu businessmen had to do something to restore the good name of Selbu.

Organization

Selbu shop owners, seeing their profits endangered by poor production, began organizing in the 1920's to demand higher quality from their knitters. Many knitters were angered and offended by the implication that their work was substandard, and at attempts to control the production. It's easy to understand how the knitters felt: You shop owners have gotten rich off our work for thirty years, and now suddenly we're not good enough for you? Over the next few years, organizers were able to convince knitters that producing goods which met consistent high standards, and were labeled as such, would yield higher profits for everyone - knitters as well as distributors. On July 8, 1934, the Selbu Husflid was formed by a coalition of 13 businesses, and a cottage was leased for the new venture's headquarters. Christening Kvennås became the first manager and Johan Hårstad acted as Chairman of the Board.

This ad for selbuvotter is from an individual merchant. The image of grinning grannies knitting your mittens is brilliant branding. It's so charming I couldn't exclude it. Courtesy of Selbu Bygdemuseum.

Husflid was not the only opportunity for knitters to sell their work. According to Annemor Sundbø, Sverre Flagestad ran a company called Selbuartikler A/S; he collected items from knitters around Selbu and then travelled around Norway selling them to souvenir shops. Selbuartikler A/S specialized in mini mittens, unwearable but adorable. Selbuartikler was in business until the 1990's.

Sverre Flagestad died in 2000 at the age of 94. Flagestad was Annemor's sister's father-in-law; I was able to contact one of his grandchildren but did not get further information before this book went to press. Other small businesses did similar work.

Selbu Husflid contracted with woolen mills to create yarns for their knitters. Namdal ullvarefabrikk produced a kind of the yarn with the name Selbugarn, special made for Selbu knitting. The knitters from Selbu also got yarn from Brødrene Krog in Røros and Alver in Åsen (Nord-Trøndelag) (Selbu Bygdemuseum) Many of the old mittens I studied used the same yarn: a smooth worsted-spun 3- or 4-ply sport weight. I assume this was selbugarn.

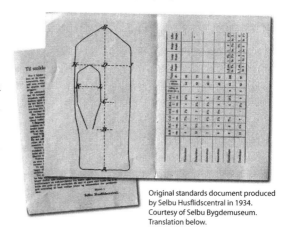

The best samples of each type of knitted article were used as models, and from them standards were created for size, weight, and so forth. Printed patterns and text would point out pitfalls: "The thumb on this pattern has thus far been too short." Items that met the new standards were marked with a special seal; those of lower quality would be returned or sold at a lower profit to the knitter. The standards were finally

Original standards document produced by Selbu Husflidscentral in 1934. Courtesy of Selbu Bygdemuseum. Translation below.

adopted when the Husflid agreed to pay each knitter a minimum of 50 kr per year; the knitter then agreed not to compete by selling her knitwear elsewhere. The organization marketed Selbu knitwear to the nation, using the image of grandmotherly country women to brand their products as wholesome, traditional, and high quality. (Selbu Bygdemuseum.)

As quality improved, so did sales. In 1935 Selbu Husflid received an interest-free loan of 10,000 kroner. In 1937 sales reached 141,128 kroner; in 1939 knitwear sales (which included over 90,000 pairs of mittens as well as socks, hats, scarves, and sweaters) topped 250,000 kroner, the equivalent of 1,000 tons of grain. These were sold not only in Norway, but across Europe and North America. Not bad business for a community of 4,000 people. (Selbu Bygdemuseum.)

While standardization helped improve quality, it reduced the number of designs that were being knit. Selbu Husflidscentral produced written patterns and preferred that knitters use them rather than original designs. Many knitters would make the same pattern over and over again, maximizing

	A-B	B-C	C-D	D-E	K-L	H-I	C-to to gusset	Cast on stitch #	Weight in gr	Index finger	Middle finger	Ring finger	Little finger
	in cm	in cm	in cm	in cm	in cm	in cm							
Man's Mittens	3.15	2.36	2.95	2.95	1.57	4.13							
	8	6	7.5	7.5	4	10.5		64	90				
Lady's Mittens	3.94	2.17	2.76	2.76	1.38	3.54							
	10	5.5	7	7	3.5	9		52	70				
Boy's Mittens	2.76	1.97	2.56	2.56	1.38	3.54							
	7	5	6.5	6.5	3.5	9		48	60				
Child's Mittens	3.15	1.57	2.17	2.17	1.18	2.95							
	8	4	5.5	5.5	3	7.5		40	45				
Man's Gloves	3.15	2.36	2.95		1.57	4.13	2.36			length 8cm	length 9.5cm	length 9cm	length 6.5cm
	8	6	7.5		4	10.5	6	64	100	width 3.5cm	width 3.5cm	width 3.5cm	width 3cm
Lady's Gloves	3.94	2.17	2.76		1.38	3.54	1.97			length 7cm	length 8cm	length 7.5cm	length 6cm
	10	5.5	7		3.5	9	5	52	90	width 3cm	width 3.5cm	width 3cm	width 2.5cm

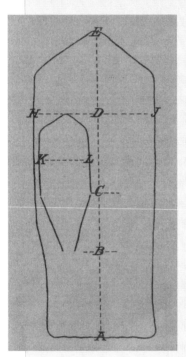

To knitters of Selbu Mittens

To help the knitters make sure the proportions of the mitten measurements come out correctly we (the board of the Selbu Home Craft Association) have made an outline of a mitten and a chart with measurements. This will indicate the average measurements for the different sizes.

The most common mistake made is that the distance between the wrist and the thumb (B-C) has been too short. This part of the mitten sometimes also comes out too narrow because there have not been enough stitches increased. Often there are too few stitches between the thumb and the edge of the mitten which causes the side border to end up on the inside (palm side) of the mitten instead of on the side when the mitten is on the hand. Make sure the thumb does not end up too short or too narrow. If the chart is followed, the mitten will have the correct size and shape.

For men and boys are the mittens and the gloves are made with a firmer wrist than the ladies and children's mittens.

On the tip of the fingers no knots can be found. Hide the knots with the help of a darning needle. In gloves, nice weaver's knots must be used, but better is to avoid knots and still make sure the ends do not come loose.

The board wishes models to be picked from the suggested collection, but other nice designs can also be used. Make sure the chosen designs coincide with the given measurements to avoid not completed designs. Make sure the borders in one mitten have a good match.

If the dyed yarn has any loose dye, wash the yarn before knitting. All the finished mittens have to be washed and dried well, preferably outside in the sun because drying them over an oven often makes the yarn turn brown. Sloppy washing destroys a product that otherwise is nice and correctly done.

The mittens have to be tied together in a way that makes it easy to try them on without untying. The mittens are tied at the top and the gloves by the wrist.

We have to ask the knitters to follow the board's instructions when it comes to choice of yarn, workmanship, groupings (mittens or gloves, sizes) and so on.

It is only by good workmanship and beautiful designs we can keep the sales up and secure our home industry. Therefore we hope all the knitters will do their best to deliver quality work. That way the knit ware from Selbu will maintain their good reputation. We will do our best to sell the products for the best possible price and profit for the producers.

The Board

Selbu Home Craft Association

Original knitting instructions from Selbu Husflidscentral, 1934. Translated by Arnhild Hillesland 2006.

their profit by mastering just a few
designs which they could reproduce
from memory, rather than creating new
designs each time. As I have written these
patterns and knit the samples, I can say
for myself that the first mitten, where the
design is being tested, takes at least 30%
longer to make than the second, which is
simply repeating what I've already done.
If I were knitting piecework to buy my
coffee, I would probably focus on one or
two designs myself, and not put in the
extra effort of creating new patterns each time.

Original pattern produced by Selbu Husflidscentral in 1934. Courtesy of Selbu Bygdemuseum.

Some knitters in Norway today, even though they knit only for family,
continue to make the same design over and over again. That's the way they
have always made mittens, so that's what they continue to do.

Even the extraordinary volume of knitted goods that Selbu created wasn't
enough to meet demand. What Selbu couldn't produce, knitters would learn
to knit for themselves.

The Evangelist

Marit Emstad may be Selbu knitting's creator, but it was another woman,
Annichen Sibbern Bøhn, who spread the gospel. Born in Oslo in 1905,
Annichen would research and preserve Norway's knitting history.

In the 1920's Annichen studied design in Oslo. In 1927 she traveled
Norway to collecting knitting designs from the countryside. With the
support of Husflid, she published her collection *Norske Strikkemønstre*
(Norwegian Knitting Designs) in 1929, and included charts for mittens,
stockings, hats, and sweaters, as well as borders, motifs, and allover patterns
that could be used on any kind of project. The book was immensely popular
and was kept in print for decades. It was translated into English in 1965,
and while it is no longer in print, old copies can be found with the help of a
used book dealer. Sundbø calls the book a "knitting bible" and credits it for
revitalizing Norway's knitting. It is the source for many of the designs in her
collection.

In the 1930's Annichen also published knitting, sewing, and embroidery
patterns in the women's weekly magazine *Urd*, and daily newspaper

Morgenbladet, using both traditional and modern design styles. *Urd* published a wide variety of articles: art and architecture reviews, craft patterns and tips, fashion advice, and advertisements for seemingly random products; stoves, beauty products, and yarns and materials for needlework. The magazine is styled similarly to American women's magazines of the time and shows Norwegian women to have sophisticated, modern taste — even those living on the farms deep in the valleys. The editors of *Morgenbladets* wrote a letter in 1930, recommending Annichen's articles, stating that they had received notes from their female readers complimenting the articles in both the content and the writing quality.

Once the Selbu style was popularized, other publishers wanted to get in on the action. Yarn mill Sandness made the publication of "traditional" patterns a major part of their business. Sometimes these patterns were created by in-house designers and named for a region, without there being an actual relationship between the design and the region. Annichen's cousin Elsa Poulsson also published knitting patterns in the 1940's, with a more modern style than Annichen's.

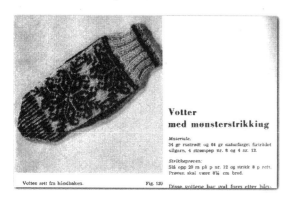

Votter med mønsterstrikking

Materiale:
34 gr rustrødt og 64 gr naturfarget firtrådet ullgarn. 4 strømpep nr. 8 og 4 nr. 12.

Strikkeprøven:
Slå opp 20 m på p nr. 12 og strikk 8 p rett. Prøven skal være 8½ cm bred.

Votten sett fra håndbaken.   Fig. 120

Disse votten har god form etter hån-

By the late 1940's the Selbuvotter style mitten and glove patterns became a common inclusion in pattern books; they were often simply titled "votter med mønsterstrikking" (mittens with design-knitting) and not identified as the Selbu style. (Bondesen, *Den Nye Strikkeboken*, 100-101) Was this was oversight, or would naming them as Selbu have been redundant?

Outside Norway they were simply called "Norwegian mittens", and the link back to their origin was severed. Elizabeth Zimmermann's *Knitter's Almanac* (page 60) offers a pattern for a "Norwegian Mitten" with no mention of Selbu. *Mary Thomas's Knitting Book* has a pattern for "Lithuanian" gloves which feature a large reindeer, a design often seen in Selbu knits but never in Baltic designs. Post-war patterns tend to use thicker yarn and needles, and the designs became necessarily coarser, lacking the fine detail of the earlier designs. This may be due to a desire on the part of the knitters to finish their projects quicker, but may also be due to the fact that it was the yarn mills that were publishing so many new patterns to sell their new yarns.

The patterns prove that women in and out of Norway wanted selbuvotter, they wanted to knit them, and they wanted to knit from a pattern. Annemor Sundbø's collection of mittens use many of Annichen's designs. The idea that all old time knitters were experts and able to create anything they wanted out of their head with never a mistake or worry, can be put into better context. Just as today, those who specialized in knitting, rather than embroidery or weaving or accounting or teaching, would have greater skill, and those who knit selbuvotter professionally got very, very good at them. But even they weren't perfect, and standards helped improve overall quality. For everyone else, a written, tested pattern was a better guarantee of quality design.

Annichen also published other books. Her first book, published before *Norske Strikkemønstre* was on children's and infants' clothing, and included sewing and knitting patterns. She also wrote a book about restyling old clothes into new ones. *Gammel till nytt* (Old to new) was very popular during the war. Annichen wrote articles and taught classes, often paid for by community groups. She also worked as an architectural assistant for her

uncle Magnus Poulsson during the time his firm created the plans for the Oslo City Hall. In her life she was highly regarded as an expert in knitting, and in 1955, when she visited one of her daughters who had emigrated to the U.S., her arrival was noted in a newspaper article. I have a copy of the article from that daughter, Annichen Kassel, but sadly the name of the paper was not included. Annichen Sibbern Bøhn died in 1978. Her daughters, Annichen (Lillen) Bøhn Kassel of Denver, and Sidsel Kringstad of Sweden, later published a booklet titled *Stikk - Knit* in honor of their mother, which was one of the first knitting books I ever purchased.

Physical evidence of the widespread popularity of Selbu knitting is found in the piles at Torridal Tweed og Ulldynefabrikk. Norway's only remaining wool recycling factory, Torridal has purchased old woolens from all over Norway for decades, shredding

Annichen's designs were used all over Norway. This photo shows many designs from Annemor Sundbø's "mitten carpet", over 1200 mittens and gloves from the piles at Torridal Tweed, Photograph courtesy Annemor Sundbø.

and recycling worn-out mittens, socks, sweaters, and so forth into new blankets. Annemor Sundbø, the factory owner, mined the piles for Norway's knitting history. Selbu mittens and gloves are among the most common and recognizable items in the piles, which mostly date from the 1930's to the 1960's, with some items from the turn of the century. Annemor published her findings in *Everyday Knitting - Treasures from the ragpile*.

The War Years and After

As it did everything else, WWII halted the knitwear business. Germany invaded Norway on April 9, 1940 and the royal family, government, and allied troops retreated to Great Britain. Many families that could, also escaped Norway and took refuge in the islands off Scotland. The Norwegian merchant fleet joined the fight against Germany.

Selbu knitting left its impact on the Fair Isle tradition when British knitters adapted variations of the selburose into their own designs. Called "Large Stars", they were introduced into Fair Isle knitting vocabulary by war refuges, and are typically seen today in the panel jerseys. The gloves and mittens shown in *Traditional Fair Isle Knitting* by Sheila McGregor display large stars on the back of the hand, checkerboard thumb gussets, small-patterned palm, and the characteristic Selbu front/back dividing line. The only thing missing is the pointy fingertip. *Traditional Fair Isle Knitting* includes many beautiful star patterns in the chart section, any of which would be at home in Selbu designs.

After the war Norway put great emphasis on recovery and industrialization. The governments plans worked even better than they had anticipated; overall economic and industrial production exceeded pre-war levels.

Industrialization even came to Selbu. Knitting machines had been available in the district since the 1920's, but it wasn't until later that they gained much ground. In 1947 Randi Kvennås purchased some old knitting machines and set them up in the Husflid basement. She hired workers to help run the machines and started producing a greater range of large items, including sweaters and cotton goods.

Output increased to meet demand, especially since skiing had grown in popularity. The factory didn't gain the widespread success of hand knitting at home, however, and closed five years after opening.

The 1960's began with sales over 1 million kroner per year, with 2000 girls and housewives producing the bulk of the products, at home or in the Husflid studio. Selbu knits were fashionable ski wear. Celebrities and Norwegian athletes posed as models and spokespersons for Selbu knits, and the organization sent about 15% of its products overseas, across Europe and to North America. (Selbu Strikkemuseum.)

Things changed by the end of the 1960's, however. Cheap imitations of poor quality hurt Selbu's marketability, Selbu knits went out of fashion and sales plummeted. Selbu Husflidscentral wanted to expand its products to appeal to the tourist market, feeling that hand knits were no longer desirable. Traditional arts and crafts were seen as lacking of creativity in many Western societies in the 1960's and 70's, so it is no wonder that they were unappreciated in Norway as well.

The idea that traditional crafts such as needlework, knitting, and woodworking are not "real" art, nor worthy of scholarly study, is an attitude that still holds in many institutions of culture today. Annemor Sundbø describes the treatment of traditional forms as unimaginative and unacceptable in art classes she took in the 1970's. Indeed, the whole stereotype of handwork, including knitting, as frivolous activity worthy only to old ladies and social misfits falls right into this frame of thinking. Only today is the image of a stereotypical knitter as an old lady in a rocking chair beginning to change, and it is the knitters who are changing it.

Sadly, this attitude took its toll on the Selbu knitting industry. With buyers preferring newly invented styles, the demand for traditional forms plummeted and the business suffered deeply.

In the early 1980's only a few elderly women were hand knitting for Selbu Husflidscentral, and the old patterns were in danger of being lost. A collection of the old patterns was compiled and new plans were made to revitalize the industry. (Selbu Husflid.) The collection booklet is available for purchase from Selbu Husflid A/S.

Husflids administrator Elizabeth Jong and consultant Eli Lunch began a campaign focused on women's fashions in 1985. The new collection would take old designs and revamp them into exciting modern fashions. The new "Original Selbu" collection received attention in and out of Norway, especially the work of knitwear designer Ellinor Flor. Fifteen machine

"...Any attempts which were not experimental or 'creative' were looked down upon."
Annemor Sundbø,
Everyday Knitting p 143

knitters were hired to produce the lines.

Selbu Husflids was poised to launch massive new marketing campaigns when production was halted due to problems with buying high-quality yarn. Additionally, controversy erupted over closed-circuit television that had been installed in the factory. The chairman resigned amid financial difficulties. In 1992 Selbu Husflidscentral filed bankruptcy. Nineteen women lost their jobs, and the district was in shock.

Merely a month later, though, the business was reformed under the name Selbu Home Industry AS with Edwin Dahlo as the new manager. Selbu Home Industry AS has eleven full time employees today, according to their website, and around 200 local knitters producing for the company.

Knitting remains a respected part of Selbu culture. The town is home to Selbu Strikkemuseum, the largest permanent knitting exhibit in Norway. Home knitters still make the traditional mittens and gloves as well as more modern garments. Selbu Home Industry AS sells its collection in a store in town and on its website under the label "Original Selbu." (Selbu Husflid.)

Selbu designs have entered the world's design library. Stars, dancers, and reindeer are commonly seen. As you study the patterns that follow and expand your research, you will discover Selbu influence on knitwear design around the world and even on the backs of fellow shoppers in the grocery store. While most people will be unaware (and uninterested) in the origin of the designs in their clothes, educated knitters will have a special connection with the past and with generations of gifted artists, those before us and those after. ❧

Technique

Before You Begin

Selbu gloves and mittens use basic techniques: knit, purl, increase, decrease, work in two colors. If you are comfortable with these, you're ready to make your first pair of selbuvotter.

For knitters who have never made a mitten or glove (*vanter* in Norwegian), I recommend first making a pair in one color. There are hundreds of simple patterns available; I like the patterns in *The Knitter's Handy Book of Patterns* by Ann Budd.

If you've never done stranded knitting, I recommend you start with a pattern that uses a stranded cuff. Knitting the cuff will give you practice maintaining your gauge and stranding tension on a plain tube of knitting before you have to do any shaping. Also, any of the mitten cuffs would make wonderful wristlets (*pulsevante* in Norwegian); just finish with a few rounds of ribbing to match the cast-on edge. I also recommend *against* weaving in the stitches as you go: weaving changes the texture of the fabric, and the contrast color (CC) color often shows between the main color (MC) stitches which muddies the design. You can twist the stranded yarn around the working yarn on long stretches, but be sure to leave plenty of slack. Two twists over the back of the hand is usually enough; the old knitters did no more than this.

The Anatomy of a Mitten

What makes a mitten a selbuvotter is the combination of structure and color design. The Selbu mitten is a masterpiece, marrying the graphic design and structural design; once the basic structure is understood, the knitter can create any kind of design imaginable, in any size or yarn. The popular eight-pointed star (selburose, or Selbu rose) can morph into snowflakes, flowers, stars; or use animal motifs or other designs.

Cuff

Selbuvotter always start at the cuff and work toward the fingertips. There is no special cast on; many of the old knitters used a knitted cast on but I have used the long-tail cast on. In my mind, the knitted on, or cabled cast on, has a wrong-side look when worked in the round, but you can use any cast on you like. The cuff is worked for 3-4" for adult sizes, 2.5-3" for children.

There are four basic styles of cuffs: ribbed, stranded, eyelet, and "fish tail" or gauntlet-style.

Ribbed cuffs are typically knit over 70-80% of the stitches necessary for the hand, and almost always they are in K2P2 ribbing, with a symmetrical stripe pattern. Ribbing keeps the cuff tight against the wrist, and are most comfortable for mittens that will be worn with a close-cuffed jacket. Ribbed cuffs can be used for any mittens, especially children's, since they tend to be the most effective at keeping out the snow. Men's mittens have tighter ribbing than women's.

Stranded cuffs typically use a pattern that is different than the main hand pattern, but it is often echoed in the thumb. Stranded cuffs generally consists of a row of stars, roses, dancers, acanthus scrolls, or other design, often surrounded by a smaller, simple pattern such as a two-stitch checkerboard. They are worked over a number of stitches close to the number needed for the lower hand, then increased or decreased to establish the right stitch count for the hand. Stranded cuffs are typically seen on men's mittens.

Eyelet cuffs create a beautiful, feminine look. Typically an open chevron pattern, with yarn-over increases to create the eyelet, these cuffs are sometimes longer than ribbing or stranded cuffs, and they often employ stripes to emphasize the movement of the stitches. Like ribbed cuffs, eyelet cuffs are often worked over much smaller stitch counts, since the eyelet will open the fabric out and have a larger gauge than stranded knitting.

Long, **Gauntlet-style cuffs** are less common, but have an especially elegant appearance. Worked in a series of stranded designs, the wide cuffs look particularly good over the sleeves of a bunad, or traditional Norwegian folk costume. They are made for girls and women.

Stitch Patterns

One of the most unusual and characteristic design features of the selbuvotter is the way the back of the hand carries one pattern, the palm a different pattern, and the two are separated by a literal dividing line. Later mittens knit at larger gauge often use just a one-stitch stripe, but older mittens often use a design I lovingly call 'dancing ants' — two solid colored one-stitch stripes surround a one-stitch alternating column. In my eyes, they look like a parade of ants marching around the top of the hand. Checkerboard lines are also popular.

Early selbuvotter used a wider range of designs than later ones show. The earlier patterns often used many design motifs; not just a star but also incidental figures such as dancing people, animals, smaller stars and asterisks, scrolls, and more, in a fine yarn to allow for many stitches. They were often but not necessarily placed symmetrically on the hand. The earliest knitters experimented widely, and the most popular styles were carried down. Over time, the design was simplified, and the stereotypical "Norwegian mitten" today is a generic Selbu style mitten with two large selburose, knit in a DK weight yarn. Norway has a tremendous variety of mitten and glove designs, unique to every valley. The Selbu style is very popular, but it is not the only style available.

Thumb Gusset

The Selbu mitten thumb gusset is a miracle of design: structure and appearance marry to create a thumb that looks and fits perfectly. Starting at the base of the hand with three stitches, the knitter increases every two, three, or four rounds, depending on gauge, and changes the color to create a characteristic checkerboard. When the checkerboard is wide enough the knitter stops increasing and the thumb stitches are set aside. Because the thumb gusset is increased 8, 10, or more stitches, the hand is necessarily narrower at the base of the thumb. When the thumb gusset is complete there should be enough stitches for the width of the palm.

Most of the old mittens show a M1 increase; just make a twisted loop on the right hand needle. Some knitters twist the right-side M1 to the right and the left side to the left to balance the gusset. Most of the old mittens just twist to the right; you can't really see the increase clearly at the small gauge after the mittens have been washed and worn a few times.

In the patterns I have specified to slip the gusset stitches onto waste yarn, then cast on a specified number of stitches for the palm and continue working the hand as charted. If the number of gusset stitches and new palm stitches are equal, you could also knit across the gusset with waste yarn, then return these stitches to the left needle and work across in the mitten yarn as if nothing had happened. If the number of gusset stitches is greater than the number for the palm, it will be necessary to use the cast-on method. I prefer the cast-on method even when the numbers are the same, because I have a hard time picking up the inside thumb in pattern from the loops of the waste-yarn method. The old knitters used either methods, so feel free to do whatever works for you.

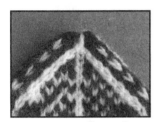

Pointed Fingertip and Thumb

Selbu mittens feature a pointed fingertip and thumb, worked outside the patterned dividing stripe. The fingertip is often longer than the wearer's hand, but they're so pretty you don't mind a bit, and this extra length also helps maintain the size: after a few washings you may find that your mittens shrink lengthwise and the pointy tip rounds out.

Arrange the stitches on the needles so that the line pattern is at the beginning of Needle 1 and the end of Needle 2. Needles 3 and 4 will contain the palm stitches.

Needle 1: Work the line pattern, ssk in MC, work the back of the hand pattern.
Needle 2: Work to two stitches before the line pattern on Needle 2, k2tog in MC, work the line pattern.
Needle 3: Ssk in MC, work the palm pattern.
Needle 4: Work the palm pattern to the last 2 sts, k2tog in MC.

Work thusly until the back or palm stitches have only 3 stitches left; then you'll work a double decrease instead of two singles: slip 1, k2tog, pass slipped stitch over. Finish the round and cut the yarn, then thread the yarn onto a tapestry needle and pull through the stitches tightly.

Often the hand back and palm have different stitch counts, and the decreases on one side of the hand will need to begin earlier than the other. In other words, if the hand back has 29 stitches and the palm has 33 stitches, the palm decreases will begin two rounds before the hand back. That way they will come out even at the fingertip.

Many of the old knitters didn't bother with this level of detail: The decreases began at the same round, and if the palm or hand back had extra stitches, so be it. They were simply finished off with the rest. Since I have the benefit of computerized charting it was easy to move the lines around until the shaping lined up perfectly.

Patterned Thumb

The thumb is patterned just as richly as the back of the hand; this means there are a lot of stitches. Most of the old mittens have big chunky thumbs; the wearers must not have minded the floppy fabric. Some knitters went down one or two needle sizes to keep reduce the gauge and make the thumb fit better.

When the hand has been worked and the fingertip finished off, the thumb is picked up from the hand and worked outward. With the mitten lying palm side up, and the fingertip pointing toward you, pick up the specified number of stitches from the cast on stitches. Pick up one stitch from the side of the thumb hole. Slip the gusset stitches back onto needles and work across them as charted. Pick up one stitch from the side of the thumb hole. There will inevitably be a hole or lose stitch at the base of the thumb, on one or both sides. Many times the old knitters just ignored them, but if they bother you, stitch them closed after the thumb is finished.

The inside thumb, coming off the palm, is worked in the same pattern as the palm. The finest mittens have been worked so that the pattern flows undisturbed from the palm to the thumb, but most have noticeable jumps in the pattern as the direction of work changes. The outside thumb is worked in a distinctive pattern that sometimes but not always echoes the stranded cuff pattern. The thumb is decreased and finished off exactly like the fingertips.

Here's a tip to make the palm pattern flow seamlessly from the hand to the inside thumb. When you cast on the new stitches, *cast on in pattern as established.* (This isn't in the charts, as they were graphically-busy already, and

I wanted to be sure they would print clearly.) Later, when you pick up the thumb stitches, pick up exactly the same colors as the cast on stitches. It feels like you're making two rows the same, but it looks perfect in the end. If it doesn't work for you, don't feel bad – only a few of the mittens I studied had perfectly flowing patterns.

Cast on new palm stitches in pattern as established ...

... and pick up inside thumb in the same colors ...

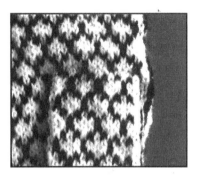

... for a perfect transition from palm to thumb.

Mutation: Gloves

Simply put, gloves are mittens with fingers.

Once you are familiar with mitten construction, it's easy to take the next step and knit gloves. The cuff, thumb, and hand are the same. When you've knit up the hand to where the fingers separate (after the first star, if you're doing a typical two selburose pattern), you'll need to divide for the fingers. The patterns for gloves have all had their finger numbers calculated, but you can use this procedure for converting any of the mitten patterns into gloves.

Look at your chart and count the number of stitches on the back of the hand and on the palm. Leave out the side patterning, the "dancing ants" for now.

Divide the hand back number and palm number by 4. That's for 4 fingers.

As an example, let's say you have 31 stitches on the back and 33 on the palm, you'll have 31÷4 and 33÷4.

31÷4 = three 8 stitch fingers and one 7 stitch fingers on the hand back.
33÷4 = three 8 stitch fingers and one 9 stitch finger on the palm.

On your hand back chart, mark 8 stitches for the pointer, middle, and ring fingers, and 7 for the pinky.

On your palm chart, mark 8 stitches for the pointer, ring, and pinky, and 9 stitches for the middle finger. It's the biggest so it needs that extra stitch.

Now that you've calculated the stitches for your fingers, it's time to knit them. Fingers are worked one at a time, starting with the pinky.

This is the second round on the pinky. Note the cast on stitches with the colored line; that's the divider between palm and back.

Work in pattern across back of the hand until you have knit the pinky fingers, including the palm stitches. Keep the pinky stitches on the needles and transfer all of the rest onto waste yarn. Adjust the needles so that the finger back is on Needle 1, the dancing ants on Needle 2, and the palm on Needle 3. On Needle 4 you will cast on extra stitches, usually from 2-4 depending on the gauge, the size of the finger, and the pattern requirements. You'll also create a stripe up the hand-side of the pinky finger, opposite the dancing ants. These will form the fabric between the pinky and the ring finger. Then join the pinky circularly and work as charted, centering the pattern on the back of the finger and maintaining the palm pattern as established on the palm side. Feel free to redistribute the stitches on the needle to make it comfortable for you. Finish off the fingertip like a pointy mitten thumb.

Next, you'll work the ring finger. Start with the stitches you cast on for the pinky. Pick up one stitch for each cast-on stitch, keeping in color pattern to create a jaunty stripe between the fingers. Transfer the ring finger stitches from the waste yarn to the needles. Cast on between the ring finger and the middle finger like you did on the pinky. Join circularly, knit the chart as before, and finish off with a nice pointy tip.

Here I've used a small crochet hook to pick up the stitches from the ones I cast on for the pinky.

The middle finger is done just the same as the ring finger; pick up the in between stitches, slip the necessary stitches from waste yarn to the needles, cast on between the middle finger and the pointer finger, join circularly, and work the chart.

The pointer finger is worked like a pinky in reverse; the thumb side "dancing ants" pattern takes the place of the cast-on stitches. You won't need to cast on any new stitches.

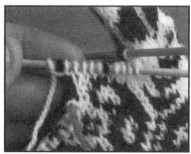

Now I've slipped the stitches from the waste yarn and cast on the new stitches between the ring finger and middle finger. I'll join in a round and make the finger.

The length of each finger is entirely up to the knitter. Some of the old gloves have all the fingers knit to the same length but wear and time have shaped them to fit the wearer's hand. Others have been knit to fit. If you have to choose between a little too long and a little too short, go with the extra length. It will shrink down with a few washings.

The thumb is worked as for a mitten.

In creating the patterns I have tried to stay true to the original, but I recommend you try on the gloves as you work and make them fit perfectly. I have had to choose between strict reproduction, working exactly to the original, and redesigning based on the original as inspiration. There are good arguments for both approaches, but I have tried to stick to actual reproduction for scholarly value. I hope you will feel confident to modify any pattern to suit yourself.

Yarn, Needles, Gauge and Size

It is always true that changing yarn and needles will change the gauge of a knitted fabric. This property is especially useful in sizing small garments like mittens.

Any pattern can be made to any size, if you use appropriate yarn and needles. If a pattern is sized for an adult and uses DK weight yarn, you can easily make them child size by substituting finer yarn and smaller needles. Likewise, the children's sizes can be made larger with heavier yarn and larger needles.

I have used Shetland wool on many of the samples, specifically because it is successful in such a wide range of gauges. The Norwegian yarns are also greatly adaptable. And yet for some reason, many of the samples have ended up fitting a Woman's Medium hand. I suspect this knitter's influence is seen here; I am a tight knitter and like to try things on as I go.

Making Your Mittens Your Own

Feel free to make gloves into mittens or mittens into gloves, change the colors, the gauge, lengthen the thumbs and fingers, modify the designs or whatever you like. Use the patterns on other garments. Folk tradition remains alive when it can grown and change to meet the current needs of its people; it becomes a lifeless ritual if held to the strictest form.

The greatest discovery I made in studying the old mittens is how the old knitters were not necessarily any more talented than we are. They followed patterns, made mistakes, corrected them — or didn't. Their stitches were occasionally too loose or too tight. Their thumb bases have holes in them. The lines between the fingers don't match up.

What they did seem to do better than we do is to accept the mistakes that they made. I have known knitters to slave, rework, rip, reknit, cry, obsess, and even throw away hundreds of dollars in yarn and needles, because they made a mistake and couldn't figure out how to Make It All Perfect. Today we have an expectation that everything we make should be neat and finished and cleanly, perfectly designed. That's because in the mass produced world, it is. Clothing manufacturers design for the machine, so the design will always perfectly "fit" the machine's capabilities.

A Selbu knitter wouldn't have thrown away a project because it wasn't perfect. She would have made what fix was practical, then continued knitting.

Selbuvotter are folk objects, not high art. A hallmark of folk art is the small mistakes and inconsistencies; they are what give a piece its life and liveliness, compared to the sleek perfection of Fine Art and mechanized production. I found a glaring mistake on the fingertip of one of my mittens, and I decided not to repair it. I think that our obsession with perfection is unhealthy, and I want knitters to feel comfortable, and to be happy with the work they do, and not criticize themselves for being imperfect. We are all imperfect, and it is our faults and flaws that make us unique and beautiful.

If you make a mistake that will haunt you and make you NOT want to wear or use something you make, then by all means, fix it. But if it doesn't haunt you, consider leaving it. Your selbuvotter will be very traditional, and your folk art will have a special spirit that no machine can reproduce. ✌

The Patterns

The patterns that follow are reproductions of actual old mittens and gloves knit in the Selbu tradition. These come from two sources: The Nordic Heritage Museum in Seattle and the private collection of Annemor Sundbø. Unfortunately, the provenance of each item is limited.

My process for recreating the patterns was this: First I measured the width, length, and gauge. I counted the number of stitches cast on. I created charts for each pattern individually, in the direction of work: the cuff, then the lower hand and thumb gusset, then the palm and fingertips for mittens, fingers for gloves, and finally the back of the thumb. I wrote first-draft patterns directly from the originals and my charts. These patterns were used by the test knitters (either me or one of twenty knitters who helped me) to create the samples. The patterns were then edited, the samples finished, washed and dried, labeled, and set aside for photography.

In writing the patterns I was often forced to decide between strictly reproducing the original or creating a new pattern based on the original, with changes made for modern knitting styles. For example, some of the gloves have fingers all the same length. I have tried to stay with strict reconstruction, for the sake of preserving historical reality rather than modify for the sake of modern tastes. With that in mind, you are encouraged to make modifications to the patterns to suit yourself. Make your fingers fit you.

Annemor #1

Source
Annemor Sundbø
Private Collection

Finished Size
Women's Medium
Length: 9.5" from cuff to fingertip
Width: 3.75" measured across palm

Yarn
Jamieson & Smith jumper weight (100% wool, 25g 105m)
MC: 1A Ecru, 2 skein
CC: 80 Dark Brown, 1 skein

Gauge
32 sts and 32 rounds = 4"/10cm measured over palm

Needles & Notions
US Size 2 (2.75mm) DPN needles or size to give gauge
Waste Yarn, Tapestry Needle

THESE UNUSUAL GLOVES USE DIFFERENT PATTERNS ON THE FINGERS, SO THAT THE HAND PATTERN CONTINUES UP TO THE FINGERTIPS. INSIDE THE CUFF HAD BEEN SEWN TWO SMALL PIECES OF WOVEN LABEL TAPE, SHOWING THE INITIALS G AND T OR POSSIBLY J. THE CUFF PATTERN IS UNASHAMEDLY INCOMPLETE IN THE ORIGINAL - LOOK AT THE SMALL PHOTO ON BOTTOM OF THE NEXT PAGE. I HAVE ROTATED THE PATTERN JUST A LITTLE; THE JOG IS NOW PLACED ON THE WRIST. SAMPLE KNIT BY IVETE TECEDOR.

Cuff

Using MC, cast on 52 sts. Divide stitches evenly onto 4 needles and join circularly, taking care not to twist stitches. Work in K2P2 ribbing 2 Rounds. Knit 1 Round MC. Work Chart A. Knit 1 Round MC, increasing one stitch — 53 sts. Work Chart B: note that this pattern DOES NOT make a complete repeat. You'll have a partial repeat. Knit 1 Round MC, increasing one stitch — 54 Sts. Work Chart C. Knit 1 Round MC thusly: * k9, M1; repeat to end of Round — 60 sts.

Lower Hand and Thumb Gusset

Begin Chart D, noting that charts are given for both Right and Left hands. Be sure to work one palm and the back for each glove; if the "other" palm gets distracting, try photocopying the page and folding over the side not in use. Work the lower hand and thumb gusset, increasing stitches as charted — 73 sts.

Set Aside Thumb

On the next Round, knit as charted until you reach the thumb, which is represented in the chart by the grey bar. Slip the 16 thumb stitches onto waste yarn and cast on 15 sts using a backward loop method. Work the rest of Chart D, which ends partway through the back of the hand.

Divide for Fingers

Notice the barred line at the top of Chart D. These lines show which stitches will be used for each finger. Slip the stitches for all stitches except the pinky finger onto waste yarn.

Pinky

Slip the pinky stitches onto 4 needles. Cast on 3 sts (MC 1, CC 1, MC 1) after the charted stitches on the back of the hand, then join the pinky finger into a Round. You will now knit only on the pinky stitches, beginning with the third stitch in the first row of the pinky chart; the first two stitches will be worked on the last two stitches cast on. Work front as shown in pinky chart; work palm side as established. Finish the tip by cutting the yarn and threading it onto the tapestry needle. Then weave it through the remaining stitches and pull tight.

Ring Finger

Slip ring finger stitches onto needles. Beginning with hand back facing you, cast on 3 sts, CC 1, MC 1, MC 1. Work across ring chart, pick up 3 sts from pinky cast-on stitches, work across palm. Continue working ring finger as charted. Finish the tip by cutting the yarn and threading it onto the tapestry needle. Then weave it through the remaining stitches and pull tight.

Middle Finger

Slip stitches from back and palm onto needles. Cast on 2 sts, CC 1, MC 1, work middle finger as charted, picking up stitches from the stitches cast on for ring finger, and working palm stitches as established, cast on 1 st in MC. Work finger as charted. Finish the tip by cutting the yarn and threading it onto the tapestry needle. Then weave it through the remaining stitches and pull tight.

Pointer Finger

Slip pointer finger stitches from hand back onto needles and work as charted (line up the side pattern in the chart with that already established), picking up 3 sts from those cast on between for the Middle finger, and join in a Round. Work pointer finger as charted. Finish the tip by cutting the yarn and threading it onto the tapestry needle. Then weave it through the remaining stitches and pull tight.

Thumb

With palm up and fingertip facing you, pick up 15 sts from the stitches you cast on earlier. Pick up 1 st from side of thumb hole. Slip stitches from waste yarn onto needles. Pick up 1 st from side of thumb hole — 33 sts. Work thumb as charted, using Chart B for the outside of the thumb, and continuing the palm pattern for the inside of the thumb. Finish the tip by cutting the yarn and threading it onto the tapestry needle. Then weave it through the remaining stitches and pull tight.

Finishing

Weave in ends on wrong side. If a small hole shows where the thumb was picked up, sew it closed using the yarn tail. Wash and block as desired.

Original gloves, Annemor Sundbø Collection

Chart A

Chart B

Chart C

Chart D

Chart E

pointer

middle

ring

pinky

pinky

ring

middle

pointer

pinky

ring

middle

pointer

pinky

ring

middle

pointer

Annemor #2

Source
Annemor Sundbø
Private Collection

Finished Size
Child's Medium
Length: 8.5" from cuff to fingertip
Width: 3.0" measured across palm

Yarn
Jamieson & Smith jumper weight (100% wool, 25g 105m)
MC: 01 White, 1 skein
CC: 29 Green, 1 skein

Gauge
32 sts and 32 rounds = 4"/10cm measured over palm

Needles & Notions
US Size 2 (2.75mm) DPN needles or size to give gauge
Waste Yarn, Tapestry Needle

THESE MITTENS ARE PERFECT TEXTBOOK EXAMPLES OF SELBU KNITTING. THE STRIPED RIBBING ON THE CUFF AND "DANCING ANTS" SEPARATOR PATTERN ARE CLASSIC, AS IS THE ELEGANTLY SHAPED THUMB GUSSET THE BACK OF THE HAND FEATURES FIR BOUGHS, WITH SMALL DIAMOND SHAPES POSITIONED IN BETWEEN. PERHAPS THEY ARE SMALL SPIDERS, WEAVING WEBS OF LOVE THROUGH THE BRANCHES, EVER GREEN. THE WHOLE APPEARANCE IS YOUNG, SWEET, CLEAN. THESE MITTENS ARE NARROW, SUITABLE FOR A GIRL. SAMPLE KNIT BY ANNE HANSEN.

Cuff

Using MC, cast on 40 sts. Divide stitches evenly onto 4 needles and join circularly, taking care not to twist stitches. Work in K2P2 ribbing as follows:

6 Rounds MC	1 Round MC
1 Round CC	1 Round CC
1 Round MC	1 Round MC
1 Round CC	1 Round CC
1 Round MC	6 Rounds MC.
1 Round CC	

Next Round increase as follows: in MC, *k5, M1; repeat to end of Round — 48 sts. Work Chart A. Knit one Round in MC.

Lower Hand and Thumb Gusset

Begin Chart B, noting that charts are given for both Right and Left hands. Be sure to work one palm and the back for each mitten; if the "other" palm gets distracting, try photocopying the page and folding over the side not in use. Work the lower hand and thumb gusset, increasing stitches as charted — 58 sts.

Set Aside Thumb

On the next Round, knit as charted until you reach the thumb, which is represented

Original mittens, Annemor Sundbø Collection

in the chart by the grey bar. Slip the 15 thumb stitches onto waste yarn and cast on 9 sts using a backward loop method — 52 sts. Work the rest of the chart, and finish the fingertip by cutting the yarn and threading it onto the tapestry needle. Then thread through the remaining stitches and pull tight.

Thumb

With palm up and fingertip facing you, pick up 9 sts from the stitches you cast on earlier. Pick up 1 st from side of thumb hole. Slip stitches from waste yarn onto needles. Pick up 1 st from side of thumb hole — 26 sts. Next Round, as you begin Chart C, decrease those stitches you picked up from the side of the thumb hole — 24 sts. Work thumb as charted, using Chart C for the outside of the thumb, and continuing the palm

pattern for the inside of the thumb. Finish the thumb tip by cutting the yarn and threading it onto the tapestry needle. Then weave it through the remaining stitches and pull tight.

Finishing

Weave in ends on wrong side. If a small hole shows where the thumb was picked up, sew it closed using the yarn tail. Wash and block mittens as desired.

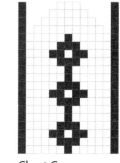

Chart A   Chart C

Chart B

Annemor #3

Source
Annemor Sundbø
Private Collection

Finished Size
Men's Medium
Length: 11.0" from cuff to fingertip
Width: 4.5" measured across palm

Yarn
Raumagarn Røros Lamullgarn (100% wool, 50g 250m)
MC: L11 Ecru, 1 skein
CC: L14 Grey, 1 skein

Gauge
35 sts and 35 rounds = 4"/10cm measured over palm

Needles & Notions
US Size 2 (2.75mm) DPN needles or size to give gauge
Waste Yarn, Tapestry Needle

In the early days, selbuvotter were often knit as gifts, and including names or initials is a time-honored tradition. These pair were knit for a man, Erling Bakke, and he seemed to enjoy them - the palm is worn right where a ski pole sits in the hand. They also feature a chain of dancers around the wrist, recalling the old chain dances that have been popular folk dances across Europe since the Middle Ages. The knitter who made these samples cleverly aligned the dancers with the stars: begin Chart A at the first stitch on the Right mitt and at the second stitch on the Left mitt. Knit Erling's name into your mittens, or feel free to personalize them with your own name.
Sample knit by Kristin Eilertsen.

Cuff

Using MC, cast on 64 sts. Divide stitches evenly onto 4 needles and join circularly, taking care not to twist stitches. Work in K2P2 ribbing as follows:

5 Rounds MC	1 Round CC
2 Rounds CC	1 Round MC
1 Round MC	1 Round CC
1 Round CC	1 Round MC
1 Round MC	2 Rounds CC
1 Round CC	5 Rounds MC.
1 Round MC	

Lower Hand and Thumb Gusset

Knit 1 Round in MC. Work Chart A. Knit 1 Round in MC, increasing as follows: Right mitt: k1, M1, k1 m1, knit rest of Round — 66 sts. Left mitt: Knit until last 2 sts, M1, k1, M1, k1 — 66 sts.

Begin Chart B, noting that charts are given for both Right and Left hands. Be sure to work one palm and the back for each mitten; if the "other" palm gets distracting, try photocopying the page and folding over the side not in use. Work the lower hand and thumb gusset, increasing stitches as charted — 80 sts.

Set Aside Thumb

On the next Round, knit as charted until you reach the thumb, which is represented in the chart by the grey bar. Slip the 17 thumb stitches onto waste yarn and cast on 17 sts using a backward loop method. Work the rest of the chart, and finish the fingertip by cutting the yarn and threading it onto the tapestry needle. Then thread through the remaining stitches and pull tight.

Thumb

With palm up and fingertip facing you, pick up 17 sts from the stitches you cast on earlier. Pick up 1 st from side of thumb hole. Slip stitches from waste yarn onto needles. Pick up 1 st from side of thumb hole — 36 sts. On First Round, decrease over the stitches picked up from the sides of the hole — 34 sts. Work thumb as charted, using Chart C. Finish the thumb tip by cutting the yarn and threading it onto the

tapestry needle. Then weave it through the remaining stitches and pull tight.

Finishing

Weave in ends on wrong side. If a small hole shows where the thumb was picked up, sew it closed using the yarn tail. Wash and block as desired.

Original mittens, Annemor Sundbø Collection

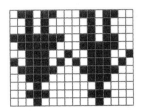

Chart A

Chart C

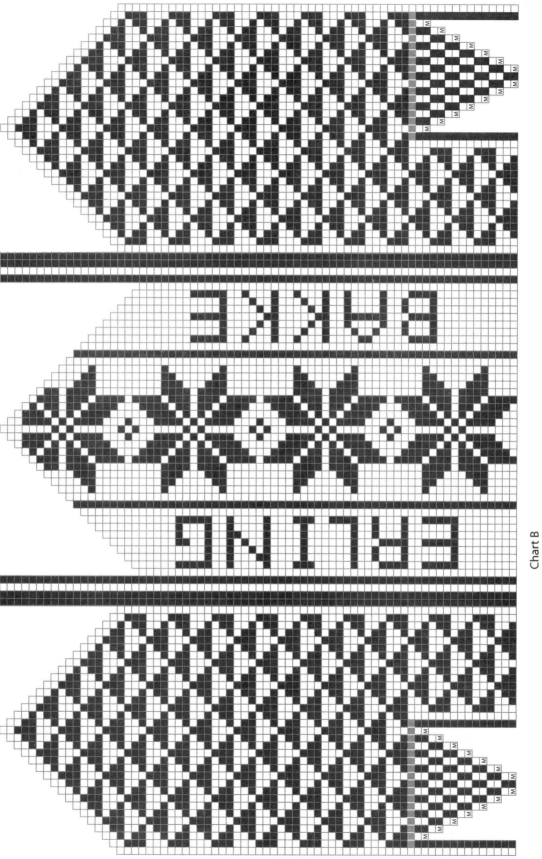

Chart B

Annemor #4

Source
Annemor Sundbø
Private Collection

Finished Size
Girls Large
Length: 10.0" from cuff to fingertip
Width: 3.5" measured across palm

Yarn
Rauma Finullgarn (100% wool, 50g 165m)
MC: 401 Ecru, 1 skein
CC: 405 Grey, 1 skein

Gauge
28 sts and 32 rounds = 4"/10cm measured over palm

Needles & Notions
US Size 3 (3.00mm) DPN needles or size to give gauge
Waste Yarn, Tapestry Needle

MANY SELBUVOTTER ARE KNIT WITH SYMMETRICAL PATTERNS; TWO LARGE STARS ON THE BACK OF THE HAND. I LOVED THESE BECAUSE OF THE JAUNTY DOG PRANCING ATOP A SNOWFLAKE. THE LACE CUFF AND SMALLER SIZE OF THE ORIGINAL INDICATE THEY WERE KNIT FOR A GIRL, BUT BIGGER GIRLS MIGHT LIKE THEM TOO. SEEN HERE IN SHETLAND JUMPER WEIGHT YARN, THE HAND IS QUITE NARROW. KNIT THEM IN A HEAVIER YARN FOR A WOMAN'S HAND. SAMPLE KNIT BY ELISABETH TOSTRUP.

Eyelet Cuff Lace (repeat of 12 sts)
Round 1: *ssk, k3, yo, k1, yo, k3, k2tog, p1; repeat from * to end.
Round 2-4: *Knit 11, Purl 1; repeat from * to end.

Repeat these 4 rounds for pattern.

Cuff
Using MC, cast on 48 sts. Divide stitches evenly onto 4 needles and join circularly, taking care not to twist stitches. Work Eyelet Cuff Lace in the following color pattern:

6 Rounds MC
2 Rounds CC
2 Rounds MC
1 Round CC
1 Round MC
1 Round CC
1 Round MC
1 Round CC
2 Rounds MC
2 Rounds CC
5 Rounds MC.

Next Round 2 Rounds in MC. Work Chart A.

Lower Hand and Thumb Gusset

Original mittens, Annemor Sundbø Collection

Knit 1 Round, increasing 2 sts — 50sts. Knit 1 Round MC. Begin Chart B, noting that charts are given for both Right and Left hands. Work the lower hand and thumb gusset, increasing stitches as charted — 56 sts.

Set Aside Thumb

On the next Round, knit as charted until you reach the thumb, which is represented in the chart by the grey bar. Slip the 11 thumb stitches onto waste yarn and cast on 11 sts using a backward loop method. Work the rest of the chart, and finish the fingertip by cutting the yarn and threading it onto the tapestry needle. Then thread through the remaining stitches and pull tight.

Thumb

With palm up and fingertip facing you, pick up 11 sts from the stitches you cast on earlier. Pick up 1 st from side of thumb hole. Slip stitches from waste yarn onto needles. Pick up 1 st from side of thumb hole — 24 sts. Work thumb as charted, using Chart B for the outside of the thumb, and continuing the palm pattern for the inside of the thumb. (Note you increase 2 sts on the first Round of the thumb chart, bringing the total thumb stitches to 26.) Finish the thumb tip by cutting the yarn and threading it onto the tapestry needle. Then weave it through the remaining stitches and pull tight.

Finishing

Weave in ends on wrong side. If a small hole shows where the thumb was picked up, sew it closed using the yarn tail. Wash and block as desired.

Chart A   Chart C

Chart B - Right Hand

Chart B - Left Hand

Annemor #5

Source
Annemor Sundbø
Private Collection

Finished Size
Child's Small
Length: 6.5" from cuff to fingertip
Width: 3.0" measured across palm

Yarn
Dalegarn Tiur (60% mohair 40% wool, 50g 126m)
MC: 020 Ecru, 1 skein
CC: 090 Black, 1 skein

Gauge
35 sts and 36 rounds = 4"/10cm measured over palm

Needles & Notions
US Size 2 (2.75mm) DPN needles or size to give gauge
Waste Yarn, Tapestry Needle

IN OLD NORSE MYTHOLOGY THE GOD ODIN HAD TWO RAVENS, MEMORY AND THOUGHT, WHO FLEW ACROSS THE LAND AND BROUGHT HIM TIDINGS OF EVENTS THROUGHOUT THE WORLD. IN MY HOME IN THE PACIFIC NORTHWEST, RAVEN IS A SHAPE-CHANGING TRICKSTER WHO PLACED THE SUN IN THE SKY AND TAUGHT THE FIRST HUMANS HOW TO HUNT AND FISH. I CHOSE DALE TIUR WITH ITS SHINY MOHAIR TO REFLECT RAVEN'S GLISTENING FEATHERS. KNIT THESE FOR ANY CHILD, A DEEP THINKER OR LAUGHING TRICKSTER, AND BRING ANCIENT SYMBOLS BACK TO LIFE.
SAMPLE KNIT BY KAREN CAMPBELL.

Cuff

Using MC, cast on 40 sts. Divide stitches evenly onto 4 needles and join circularly, taking care not to twist stitches. Work in K2P2 ribbing for 2 Rounds. Knit 2 Rounds in MC. Work Chart A.

Next Round in MC, increase as follows: *k5, M1; repeat to end of Round — 48 sts. Knit one rounds in MC.

Lower Hand and Thumb Gusset

Begin Chart B, noting that charts are given for both Right and Left hands. Be sure to work one palm and the back for each mitten; if the "other"

palm gets distracting, try photocopying the page and folding over the side not in use. Work the lower hand and thumb gusset, increasing stitches as charted — 54 sts.

Set Aside Thumb

On the next Round, knit as charted until you reach the thumb, which is represented in the chart by the grey bar. Slip the 11 thumb stitches onto waste

Original mittens, Annemor Sundbø Collection

yarn and cast on 5 sts using a backward loop method. Work the rest of the chart, and finish the fingertip by cutting the yarn and threading it onto the tapestry needle. Then thread through the remaining stitches and pull tight.

Thumb

With palm up and fingertip facing you, pick up 5 sts from the stitches you cast on earlier. Pick up 2 sts from side of thumb hole. Slip stitches from waste yarn onto needles. Pick up 1 st from side of thumb hole — 19 sts. Work thumb as charted, using Chart C for the outside of the thumb, and continuing the palm pattern for the inside of the thumb. Finish the thumb tip by cutting the yarn and threading it onto the tapestry needle. Then weave it through the remaining stitches and pull tight.

Finishing

Weave in ends on wrong side. If a small hole shows where the thumb was picked up, sew it closed using the yarn tail. Wash and block as desired.

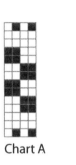

Chart A

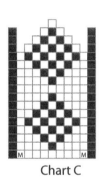

Chart C

Chart B

Annemor #6

Source
Annemor Sundbø
Private Collection

Finished Size
Girl's Large or Women's Small
Length: 10.0" from cuff to fingertip
Width: 3.5" measured across palm

Yarn
Raumagarn Gammelserie (100% wool 50g 160m)
MC: 401 Ecru, 1 skein
CC: 436 Black, 1 skein

Gauge
28 sts and 32 rounds = 4"/10cm measured over palm

Needles & Notions
US Size 2 (2.75mm) DPN needles or size to give gauge
Waste Yarn, Tapestry Needle

IF THERE WAS ANY DOUBT WHETHER WOMEN COULD WEAR MOOSE PATTERNS, THESE GLOVES SHOULD PUT IT TO REST. THE LACY WRIST SHOWS THESE ARE CLEARLY DESIGNED FOR A WOMAN, AND THE ORIGINAL WOOL IS SOFT AND COZY. THE PALM AND INSIDE FINGERS HAVE BEEN WORN THROUGH AND ARE WOVEN; THESE REPAIRS ARE ALSO WORN, SO IT'S OBVIOUS THAT THE WEARER REALLY LOVED HER GLOVES. THE KNITTER USED THE SAME DESIGN FOR EACH FINGER, BUT THE LENGTHS VARY; FEEL FREE TO FINISH THEM OFF AT A LENGTH THAT'S COMFORTABLE.
SAMPLE KNIT BY MICHELLE MOLIS.

Eyelet Cuff Lace (repeat of 12 sts)
Round 1: *ssk, k3, yo, k1, yo, k3, k2tog, p1;
repeat from * to end.
Round 2-4: *k11, p1; repeat from * to end.

Repeat these 4 Rounds for pattern.

Cuff
Cast on 44 sts using long tailed method over two needles. Divide stitches evenly onto 4 needles. Join circularly, taking care not to twist stitches. Knit six Rounds. Next Round, fold the hem to the inside (purl side) and pick up stitch through the stitch on the needle AND through the cast-

on stitch rows below it. Pull new stitch through both to join the edge to the work.

Work Eyelet Cuff Lace in the following color pattern:

4 rounds MC	2 rounds MC
3 rounds CC	3 rounds CC
2 rounds MC	4 rounds MC
1 rounds CC	

Knit 1 Round in MC, increasing every 4 sts 10 times — 54 sts. Work Chart A.

Lower Hand and Thumb Gusset

Begin Chart B, noting that charts are given for both Right and Left hands. Be sure to work one palm and the back for each glove; if the "other" palm gets distracting, try photocopying the page and folding over the side not in use. Work the lower hand and thumb gusset, increasing stitches as charted — 64 sts.

Set Aside Thumb

On the next Round, knit as charted until you reach the thumb, which is represented in the chart by the grey bar. Slip the 14 thumb stitches onto waste yarn and cast on 14 sts using a backward loop method. Work the rest of Chart B.

Divide for Fingers

Notice the barred line at the top of Chart B. These lines show which stitches will be used for each finger. Work the back of the hand stitches in MC. Work across the pinky fingers in pattern on the palm. Slip all stitches except the pinky finger onto waste yarn.

Pinky

Slip the pinky stitches onto 2 needles. Cast on 4 sts after the charted stitches on the back of the hand, then join the pinky finger into a Round. You will now knit only on the pinky stitches, beginning with the first row of Chart C. Work palm side as established. Finish the tip by cutting the yarn and threading it onto the tapestry needle. Then weave it through the remaining stitches and pull tight.

Ring Finger

Slip ring finger stitches onto needles. Beginning with hand back facing you, cast on 4 sts. Work across hand back using Chart C, pick up 4 sts from pinky cast-on stitches, work across palm. Continue working ring finger as Chart C. Finish the tip by cutting the yarn and threading it onto the tapestry needle. Then weave it through the remaining stitches and pull tight.

Middle Finger

Slip stitches from back and palm onto needles. Cast on 4 sts, work middle finger as Chart C, picking up stitches from the stitches cast on for ring finger, and working palm stitches as established. Work finger as charted. Finish the tip by cutting the yarn and threading it onto the tapestry needle. Then weave it through the remaining stitches and pull tight.

Pointer Finger

Slip pointer finger stitches from hand back onto needles and work as Chart C (line up the side pattern in the chart with that already established), picking up 4 sts from those cast on between for the middle finger, and join in a Round. Work pointer finger as Chart C. Finish the tip by cutting the yarn and threading it onto the tapestry needle. Then weave it through the remaining stitches and pull tight.

Thumb

With palm up and fingertip facing you, pick up 14 sts from the stitches you cast on earlier. Pick up 1 st from side of thumb hole. Slip stitches from waste yarn onto needles and begin Chart D. Pick up 1 st from side of thumb hole — 30 sts. Work thumb as charted, using Chart D for the outside of the thumb, and continuing the palm pattern for the inside of the thumb.

Original gloves, Annemor Sundbø Collection

53

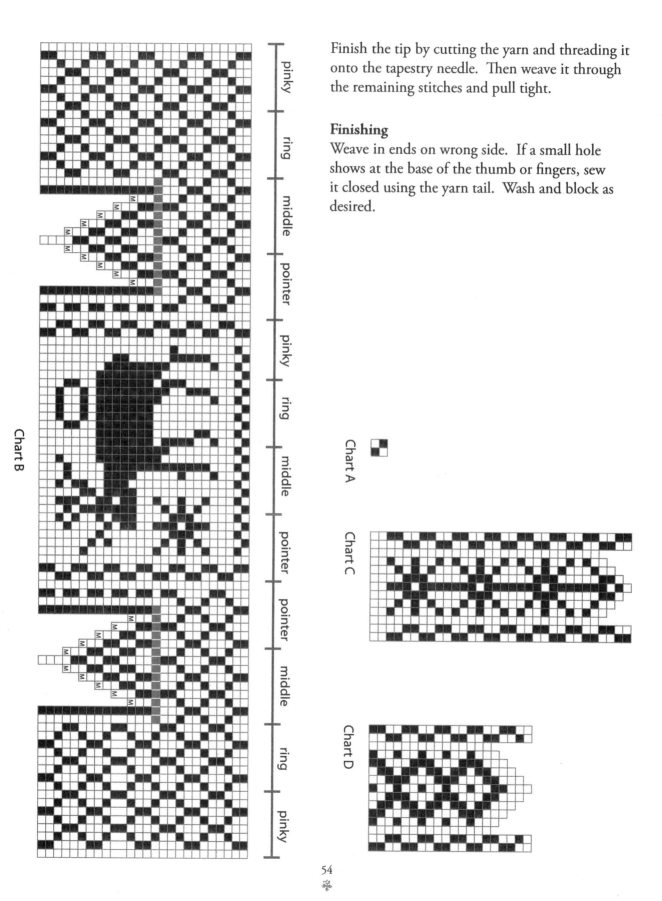

Finish the tip by cutting the yarn and threading it onto the tapestry needle. Then weave it through the remaining stitches and pull tight.

Finishing
Weave in ends on wrong side. If a small hole shows at the base of the thumb or fingers, sew it closed using the yarn tail. Wash and block as desired.

Chart A

Chart B

Chart C

Chart D

Annemor #7

Source
Annemor Sundbø
Private Collection

Finished Size
Men's Medium or Women's Large
Length: 10.0" from cuff to fingertip
Width: 3.5" measured across palm

Yarn
Raumagarn Gammelserie (100% wool 50g 160m)
MC: 401 Ecru, 1 skein
CC: 436 Black, 1 skein

Gauge
28 sts and 32 rounds = 4"/10cm measured over palm

Needles & Notions
US Size 2 (2.75mm) DPN needles or size to give gauge
Waste Yarn, Tapestry Needle

THE EDDAS TELL OF YGGDRASIL, THE TREE THAT SUPPORTS THE WORLD, AND THE FOUR STAGS THAT FEED ON ITS SHOOTS AND BARK. THE REINDEER HERE IS NIBBLING ON A SPROUT, REMINDING US OF THE ANCIENT STORY. THESE ARE LARGE GLOVES, ORIGINALLY SIZED AND STYLED FOR A MAN, BUT AS YOU KNOW NOW, ANY PATTERN CAN BE RE SIZED BY CHANGING THE YARN AND NEEDLES. SAMPLE KNIT BY WENDY COLBERT.

Cuff
Using MC, cast on 60 sts. Divide stitches evenly onto 4 needles. Join circularly, taking care not to twist stitches. Work in K1P1 ribbing for 3 Rounds. Knit 3 Rounds. Work Chart A. Knit 3 Round in MC; on the second Round increase every 6 sts 9 times — 69 sts.

Lower Hand and Thumb Gusset
Begin Chart B, noting that charts are given for both Right and Left hands. Work the lower hand and thumb gusset, increasing stitches as charted — 79 sts.

Set Aside Thumb
On the next Round, knit as charted until you reach the thumb, which is represented in the chart by the grey bar. Slip the 15 thumb stitches onto waste yarn and cast on 11 sts using a backward loop method. Work the rest of Chart B.

Divide for Fingers
Notice the barred line at the top of Chart B. These lines show which stitches will be used for each finger. Work the back of the hand stitches in MC. Work across the pinky fingers on the palm. Slip the stitches for all stitches except the pinky finger onto waste yarn.

Pinky

Slip the pinky stitches onto 4 needles. Cast on 2 sts after the charted stitches on the back of the hand, then join the pinky finger into a Round. You will now knit only on the pinky stitches, beginning with the first row of Chart C. Work palm side as established. Finish the tip by cutting the yarn and threading it onto the tapestry needle. Then weave it through the remaining stitches and pull tight.

Ring Finger

Slip ring finger stitches onto needles. Beginning with hand back facing you, cast on 2 sts. Work across ring chart, pick up 2 sts from pinky cast-on stitches, work across palm as established. Continue working ring finger as charted. Finish the tip by cutting the yarn and threading it onto the tapestry needle. Then weave it through the remaining stitches and pull tight.

Middle Finger

Slip stitches from back and palm onto needles. Cast on 2 sts, work middle finger as charted, picking up stitches from the stitches cast on for ring finger, and work palm stitches as established. Work finger as charted. Finish the tip by cutting the yarn and threading it onto the tapestry needle. Then weave it through the remaining stitches and pull tight.

Pointer Finger

Slip pointer finger stitches from hand back onto needles and work as charted (line up the side pattern in the chart with that already established), picking up 2 sts from those cast on between for the Middle finger, and join in a Round. Work pointer finger as charted. Finish the tip by cutting the yarn and threading it onto the tapestry needle. Then weave it through the remaining stitches and pull tight.

Thumb

With palm up and fingertip facing you, pick up 11 sts from the stitches you cast on earlier. Pick up 1 st from side of thumb hole. Slip stitches from waste yarn onto needles. Pick up 1 st from side of thumb hole — 28 sts. Work thumb as charted, using Thumb for the outside of the thumb, and continuing the palm pattern for the inside of the thumb. Finish the tip by cutting the yarn and threading it onto the tapestry needle. Then weave it through the remaining stitches and pull tight.

Finishing

Weave in ends on wrong side. If a small hole shows at the base of the thumb or fingers, sew it closed using the yarn tail. Wash and block as desired.

Original gloves, Annemor Sundbø Collection

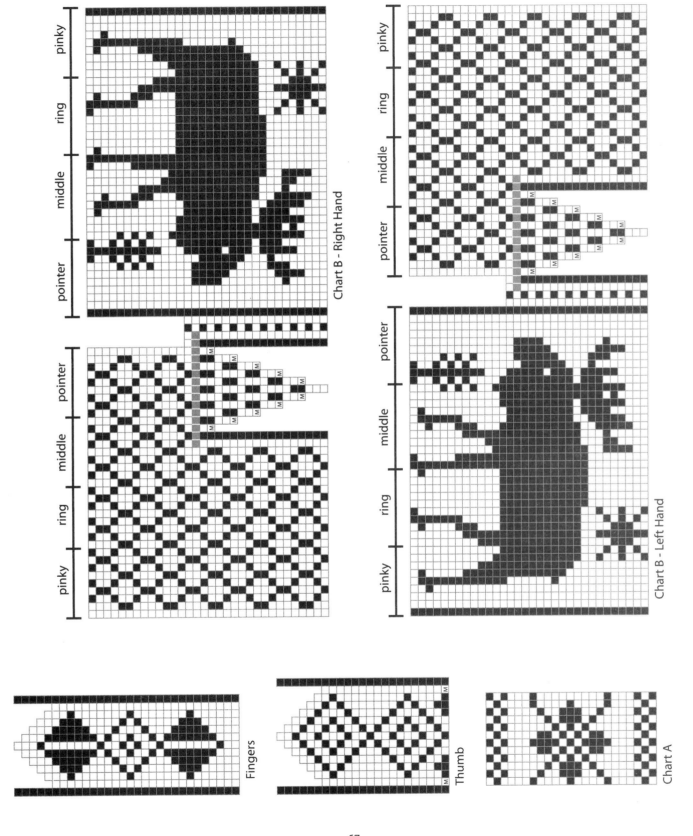

Chart B - Right Hand

Chart B - Left Hand

Fingers

Thumb

Chart A

Annemor #8

Source
Annemor Sundbø
Private Collection

Finished Size
Women's Medium or Men's Small
Length: 9.0" from cuff to fingertip
Width: 4.0" measured across palm

Yarn
Jamieson & Smith jumper weight (100% wool, 25g 105m)
MC: 1A Ecru, 2 skeins
CC: 93 Red, 1 skein

Gauge
33 sts and 34 rounds = 4"/10cm measured over palm

Needles & Notions
US Size 2 (2.75mm) DPN needles or size to give gauge
Waste Yarn, Tapestry Needle

I LOVE THE UNUSUAL DESIGN OF THE CENTRAL STAR SEEN HERE; UNLIKE MOST, IT IS NOT BASED ON THE SELBUROSE BUT HAS ITS OWN MATHEMATICAL PATTERN. THE LINES THAT COME OUT FROM THE CORNERS ARE PINE BOUGHS, AND THEY ARE SEEN AGAIN ON THE FINGERS. THE CUFF MIGHT BE A LITTLE SHORT FOR A MAN'S WRIST. JUST ADD ANOTHER BAND OF PATTERN TO LENGTHEN; SYMMETRY NOT NEEDED. MAKE THE FINGERS AS LONG AS YOU LIKE, BUT BE WARNED THAT THIS PAIR USED ALL BUT ONE YARD OF A SINGLE SKEIN OF CC. SAMPLE KNIT BY KAREN WALTER.

Cuff

Using MC, cast on 60 sts. Divide stitches evenly onto 4 needles. Join circularly, taking care not to twist stitches. Work in K1P1 ribbing for 4 Rounds. Knit 1 Round. Work Chart A. Knit 2 Rounds in MC.

Lower Hand and Thumb Gusset

Begin Chart B, noting that charts are given for both Right and Left hands. Be sure to work one palm and the back for each glove; if the "other" palm gets distracting, try photocopying the page and folding over the side not in use. Work the lower hand and thumb gusset, increasing stitches as charted — 76 sts.

Set Aside Thumb

On the next Round, knit as charted until you reach the thumb, which is represented in the chart by the grey bar. Slip the 17 thumb stitches onto waste yarn and cast on 17 sts using a backward loop method. Work the rest of Chart B.

Divide for Fingers

Notice the barred line at the top of Chart B. These lines show which stitches will be used for each finger. Work the back of the hand stitches in MC. Work across the pinky fingers on the palm. Slip the stitches for all stitches except the pinky finger onto waste yarn.

Pinky

Slip the pinky stitches onto 4 needles. Cast on 4 sts after the charted stitches on the back of the hand, then join the pinky finger into a Round. You will now knit only on the pinky stitches, beginning with the first row of Finger chart. Work palm side as established. Finish the tip by cutting the yarn and threading it onto the tapestry needle. Then weave it through the remaining stitches and pull tight.

Ring Finger

Slip ring finger stitches onto needles. Beginning with hand back facing you, cast on 3 sts. Work across Finger chart, picking up 4 sts from pinky cast-on stitches, and working across palm as established. Continue working ring finger as charted. Finish the tip by cutting the yarn and threading it onto the tapestry needle. Then weave it through the remaining stitches and pull tight.

Middle Finger

Slip middle finger stitches onto needles. Beginning with hand back facing you, cast on 2 sts. Work across Finger chart, picking up 3 sts from the stitches cast on for ring finger, and working across palm as established. Continue working middle finger as charted. Finish the tip by cutting the yarn and threading it onto the tapestry needle. Then weave it through the remaining stitches and pull tight.

Pointer Finger

Slip pointer finger stitches from hand back onto needles and work as charted (line up the side pattern in the chart with that already

established), picking up 3 sts from those cast on between for the middle finger. Work pointer finger as charted. Finish the tip by cutting the yarn and threading it onto the tapestry needle. Then weave it through the remaining stitches and pull tight.

Thumb

With palm up and fingertip facing you, pick up 15 sts from the stitches you cast on earlier. Pick up 1 st from side of thumb hole. Slip stitches from waste yarn onto needles and begin Thumb chart. Pick up 1 st from side of thumb hole — 32 sts. Next Round, decrease over the two stitches picked up from the side of the hole while working thumb as charted, and continue the palm pattern as established for the inside of the thumb. Finish the tip by cutting the yarn and threading it onto the tapestry needle. Then weave it through the remaining stitches and pull tight.

Finishing

Weave in ends on wrong side. If a small hole shows at the base of the thumb or fingers, sew it closed using the yarn tail. Wash and block as desired.

Original gloves, Annemor Sundbø Collection

Chart A

Chart B

Finger

Thumb

Annemor #9

Source
Annemor Sundbø
Private Collection

Finished Size
Men's Medium
Length: 9.5" from cuff to fingertip
Width: 4.0" measured across palm

Yarn
Jamieson & Smith jumper weight (100% wool, 25g 105m)
MC: 1A Ecru, 1 skein
CC: 54 Grey, 1 skein

Gauge
32 sts and 32 rounds = 4"/10cm measured over palm

Needles & Notions
US Size 2 (2.75mm) DPN needles or size to give gauge
Waste Yarn, Tapestry Needle

I AM NOT CONVINCED THESE MITTENS ARE ORIGINALLY FROM SELBU. THEY LACK CERTAIN CHARACTERISTIC FEATURES: THE "DANCING ANTS", THE PATTERNED THUMB, THE PALM AND BACK OF HAND ARE WORKED IN THE SAME PATTERN, THE GUSSET IS WORKED IN STRIPES RATHER THAN THE TYPICAL CHECKERBOARD. THEY ARE SIMILAR TO A DESIGN IN NORWEGIAN KNITTING DESIGNS, WHICH BØHN IDENTIFIES AS COMING FROM JÆREN. I DECIDED TO INCLUDE THEM ANYWAY BECAUSE THEY ARE UNUSUAL. IF YOU KNOW SOMEONE WITH SQUARE HANDS, THESE MIGHT FIT PERFECTLY. SAMPLE KNIT BY VANESSA GRIMMETT.

Cuff
Using MC, cast on 64 sts. Divide stitches evenly onto 4 needles and join circularly, taking care not to twist stitches. Work in K2P2 ribbing for 3 Rounds. Knit 1 Round in MC. Work Chart A. Knit 1 Round in MC, decreasing 2 sts — 62 sts.

Lower Hand and Thumb Gusset
Begin Chart B, noting that charts are given for both Right and Left hands. Be sure to work one palm and the back for each mitten; if the "other" palm gets distracting, try photocopying the page and folding over the side not in use. Since this pattern doesn't have the typical "dancing ants"

divider pattern, I recommend you make a note on the chart to show where the palm and hand back are divided. Work the lower hand and thumb gusset, increasing stitches as charted — 72 sts.

Set Aside Thumb
On the next Round, knit as charted until you reach the thumb, which is represented in the chart by the grey bar. Slip the 16 thumb stitches onto waste yarn and cast on 16 sts using a backward loop method. Work the rest of the chart, and finish the fingertip by cutting the yarn and threading it onto the tapestry needle. Then thread through the remaining stitches and pull tight.

Thumb

With palm up and fingertip facing you, pick up 16 sts from the stitches you cast on earlier. Pick up 1 st from side of thumb hole. Slip stitches from waste yarn onto needles. Pick up 1 st from side of thumb hole — 34 sts. Work thumb in checkerboard as established, until thumb measures 2.5" or desired length. Decrease as for fingertips.

Finishing

Weave in ends on wrong side. If a small hole shows where the thumb was picked up, sew it closed using the yarn tail. Wash and block as desired.

Original mittens, Annemor Sundbø Collection

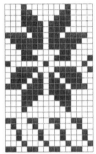

Chart A

Chart B

Annemor #10

Source
Annemor Sundbø
Private Collection

Finished Size
Men's Medium or Women's Large
Length: 10.0" from cuff to fingertip
Width: 3.5" measured across palm

Yarn
Raumagarn Gammelserie (100% wool 50g 160m)
MC: 401 Ecru, 1 skein
CC: 436 Black, 1 skein

Gauge
28 sts and 32 rounds = 4"/10cm measured over palm

Needles & Notions
US Size 2 (2.75mm) DPN needles or size to give gauge
Waste Yarn, Tapestry Needle

HERE ARE SOME WONDERFUL MEN'S GLOVES THAT ACTUALLY TURNED OUT TO FIT A MAN. HATS OFF TO THE KNITTER. THE VERY UNUSUAL SPIKY STAR PATTERN LOOKS GREAT WITH THE MODIFIED SELBUROSE SEEN ON THE CUFF, FINGERS, AND THUMB. I SUSPECT THIS DESIGN IS FROM A HUSFLID PATTERN, OR AT LEAST MADE BY A VERY EXPERIENCED SELBUVOTTER KNITTER. SAMPLE KNIT BY HOLLY ODEGARD.

Cuff
Using MC, cast on 60 sts. Divide stitches evenly onto 4 needles. Join circularly, taking care not to twist stitches. Work in K1P1 ribbing for 1 Round. Knit 1 Rounds. Work Chart A. Knit 2 Round in MC. Work Chart B. Knit 2 Rounds in MC. Work Chart A. Knit 2 Rounds in MC.

Lower Hand and Thumb Gusset
Begin Chart C, noting that charts are given for both Right and Left hands. Be sure to work one palm and the back for each mitten; if the "other" palm gets distracting, try photocopying the page and folding over the side not in use. Work the lower hand and thumb gusset, increasing stitches as charted — 68 sts.

Set Aside Thumb
On the next Round, knit as charted until you reach the thumb, which is represented in the chart by the grey bar. Slip the 14 thumb stitches onto waste yarn and cast on 14 sts using a backward loop method. Work the rest of Chart C.

Divide for Fingers
Notice the barred line at the top of Chart C. These lines show which stitches will be used for each finger. Work the back of the hand stitches in MC. Work across the pinky fingers on the palm. Slip the stitches for all stitches except the pinky finger onto waste yarn.

Pinky

Slip the pinky stitches onto 4 needles. Cast on 4 sts after the charted stitches on the back of the hand, then join the pinky finger into a Round. You will now knit only on the pinky stitches, beginning with the first row of Chart D. Work palm side as established. Finish the tip by cutting the yarn and threading it onto the tapestry needle. Then weave it through the remaining stitches and pull tight.

Ring Finger

Slip ring finger stitches onto needles. Beginning with hand back facing you, cast on 4 sts. Work across Chart D, pick up 4 sts from pinky cast-on stitches, and work palm as established. Continue working ring finger as charted. Finish the tip by cutting the yarn and threading it onto the tapestry needle. Then weave it through the remaining stitches and pull tight.

Middle Finger

Slip stitches from back and palm onto needles. Cast on 4 sts, work middle finger as Chart D, picking up 4 sts from the stitches cast on for ring finger, and work palm stitches as established. Work finger as charted. Finish the tip by cutting the yarn and threading it onto the tapestry needle. Then weave it through the remaining stitches and pull tight.

Pointer Finger

Slip pointer finger stitches from hand back onto needles and work as charted (line up the side pattern in the chart with that already established), picking up 4 sts from those cast on between for the Middle finger, and join in a Round. Work pointer finger as Chart D. Finish the tip by cutting the yarn and threading it onto the tapestry needle. Then weave it through the remaining stitches and pull tight.

Thumb

With palm up and fingertip facing you, pick up 14 sts from the stitches you cast on earlier. Pick up 1 st from side of thumb hole. Slip stitches from waste yarn onto needles. Pick up 1 st from side of thumb hole — 30 sts. Work thumb as charted, using Chart D for the outside of the thumb, and continuing the palm pattern for the inside of the thumb. Finish the tip by cutting the yarn and threading it onto the tapestry needle. Then weave it through the remaining stitches and pull tight.

Finishing

Weave in ends on wrong side. If a small hole shows at the base of the thumb or fingers, sew it closed using the yarn tail. Wash and block as desired.

Original gloves, Annemor Sundbø Collection

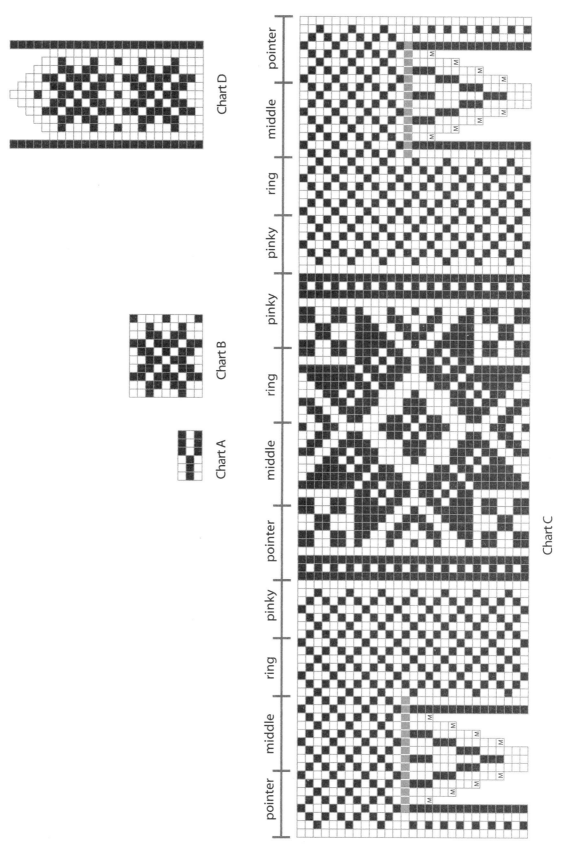

Chart D

Chart B

Chart A

Chart C

Annemor #11

Source
Annemor Sundbø
Private Collection

Finished Size
Women's Medium or Men's Small
Length: 10.0" from cuff to fingertip
Width: 4.0" measured across palm

Yarn
Jamieson & Smith jumper weight (100% wool, 25g 105m)
MC: 1A Ecru, 1 skein
CC: 54 Grey, 1 skein

Gauge
32 sts and 32 rounds = 4"/10cm measured over palm

Needles & Notions
US Size 2 (2.75mm) DPN needles or size to give gauge
Waste Yarn, Tapestry Needle

ANOTHER PAIR OF MEN'S GLOVES, THIS TIME WITH A SELBUROSE MORPHED INTO A FOUR-LEAF CLOVER. THE CLOVER COULD BE A CHARM TO BRING THE WEARER GOOD LUCK, OR COULD REPRESENT CHRIST; NOTE ALSO THE SMALL CROSSES AT EACH OF THE FOUR CORNERS. THE CUFF, FINGERS, AND THUMB USE THE CHAINED ROSE DESIGN. PERHAPS THESE GLOVES WERE MADE WITH THE INTENTION OF BRINGING THE WEARER GOOD LUCK IN LOVE, OR AS A POTENT SYMBOL OF CHRIST'S LOVE FOR THE CHURCH. THESE SAMPLES KNIT UP TO FIT A WOMAN'S HAND ON US SIZE 2; TRY SIZE 3 FOR MEN'S. SAMPLE KNIT BY ANGELA HO.

Cuff

Using MC, cast on 60 sts. Divide stitches evenly onto 4 needles. Join circularly, taking care not to twist stitches. Work in K1P1 ribbing for 3 Rounds. Work Chart A. Knit 2 Round in MC.

Lower Hand and Thumb Gusset

Begin Chart B, noting that charts are given for both Right and Left hands. Be sure to work one palm and the back for each mitten; if the "other" palm gets distracting, try photocopying the page and folding over the side not in use. Work the lower hand and thumb gusset, increasing stitches as charted — 70 sts.

Set Aside Thumb

On the next Round, knit as charted until you reach the thumb, which is represented in the chart by the grey bar. Slip the 13 thumb stitches onto waste yarn and cast on 13 sts using a backward loop method. Work the rest of Chart B.

Divide for Fingers

Notice the barred line at the top of Chart B.

These lines show which stitches will be used for each finger. Work the back of the hand stitches in MC. Work across the pinky fingers on the palm. Slip the stitches for all stitches except the pinky finger onto waste yarn.

Pinky

Slip the pinky stitches onto 4 needles. Cast on 3 sts after the charted stitches on the back of the hand, then join the pinky finger into a Round. You will now knit only on the pinky stitches, beginning with the first row of Chart C. Work palm side as established. Finish the tip by cutting the yarn and threading it onto the tapestry needle. Then weave it through the remaining stitches and pull tight.

Ring Finger

Slip ring finger stitches onto needles. Beginning with hand back facing you, cast on 3 sts. Work across Chart C, pick up 3 sts from pinky cast-on stitches, work across palm. Continue working ring finger as charted. Finish the tip by cutting the yarn and threading it onto the tapestry needle. Then weave it through the remaining stitches and pull tight.

Middle Finger

Slip stitches from back and palm onto needles. Cast on 3 sts, work middle finger as Chart C, picking up 3 sts from the stitches cast on for ring finger, and work palm stitches as established. Work finger as charted. Finish the tip by cutting the yarn and threading it onto the tapestry needle. Then weave it through the remaining stitches and pull tight.

Pointer Finger

Slip pointer finger stitches from hand back onto needles and work as Chart C (line up the side pattern in the chart with that already established) , picking up 3 sts from those cast on between for the Middle finger, and join in a Round. Work pointer finger as charted. Finish the tip by cutting the yarn and threading it onto the tapestry needle. Then weave it through the remaining stitches and pull tight.

Thumb

With palm up and fingertip facing you, pick up 13 sts from the stitches you cast on earlier. Pick up 1 st from side of thumb hole. Slip stitches from waste yarn onto needles. Pick up 1 st from side of thumb hole — 28 sts. Work thumb as charted, using Chart D for the outside of the thumb, and continuing the palm pattern for the inside of the thumb. Finish the tip by cutting the yarn and threading it onto the tapestry needle. Then weave it through the remaining stitches and pull tight.

Finishing

Weave in ends on wrong side. If a small hole shows at the base of the thumb or fingers, sew it closed using the yarn tail. Wash and block as desired.

Original gloves, Annemor Sundbø Collection

Chart B

Chart A

Chart C

Chart D

Annemor #12

Source
Annemor Sundbø
Private Collection

Finished Size
Women's Large or Men's Small
Length 10.25" from cuff to fingertip
Width: 4.0" measured across palm

Yarn
Raumagarn Gammelserie (100% wool 50g 160m)
MC: 401 Ecru, 1 skein
CC: 436 Black, 1 skein

Gauge
32 sts and 33 rounds = 4"/10cm measured over palm

Needles & Notions
US Size 2 (2.75mm) DPN needles or size to give gauge
Waste Yarn, Tapestry Needle

THESE GLOVES ARE BEAUTIFULLY BALANCED IN DESIGN; I SUSPECT THEY MAY HAVE BEEN KNIT FROM A HUSFLID PATTERN. NOTE HOW THE FINGER PATTERN AND THE THUMB PATTERN ARE RELATED. THE CUFF PATTERN EVEN MATCHES UP WITH THE STITCH COUNT. THE FINGERS ARE A LITTLE LONG; FOR WOMEN'S SIZE FEEL FREE TO SHORTEN THEM. I THINK THE MAIN STAR WOULD BE BEAUTIFUL AS A LARGE REPEAT, OVER A SWEATER OR EVEN A BLANKET. HOW LUXURIOUS WOULD THAT BE? SAMPLE KNIT BY PAT MARTIN.

Cuff
Using MC, cast on 60 sts. Divide stitches evenly onto 4 needles. Join circularly, taking care not to twist stitches. Work in K1P1 ribbing for 3 Rounds. Work Chart A. Knit 2 Round in MC.

Lower Hand and Thumb Gusset
Begin Chart B, noting that charts are given for both Right and Left hands. Be sure to work one palm and the back for each mitten; if the "other" palm gets distracting, try photocopying the page and folding over the side not in use. Work the lower hand and thumb gusset, increasing stitches as charted — 72 sts.

Set Aside Thumb
On the next Round, knit as charted until you reach the thumb, which is represented in the chart by the grey bar. Slip the 17 thumb stitches onto waste yarn and cast on 17 sts using a backward loop method. Work the rest of Chart B.

Divide for Fingers
Notice the barred line at the top of Chart B. These lines show which stitches will be used for each finger. Work the back of the hand stitches in MC. Work across the pinky fingers on the palm. Slip the stitches for all stitches except the pinky finger onto waste yarn.

Pinky
Slip the pinky stitches onto 4 needles. Cast on 3 sts after the charted stitches on the back of the hand, then join the pinky finger into a Round. You will now knit only on the pinky stitches, beginning with the first row of Chart C - Pointers & Pinkies. Work palm side as established. Finish the tip by cutting the yarn and threading it onto the tapestry needle. Then weave it through the remaining stitches and pull tight.

Ring Finger
Slip ring finger stitches onto needles. Beginning with hand back facing you, cast on 3 sts. Work across Chart C, pick up 3 sts from pinky cast-on stitches, work across palm. Continue working ring finger as charted. Finish the tip by cutting the yarn and threading it onto the tapestry needle. Then weave it through the remaining stitches and pull tight.

Middle Finger
Slip stitches from back and palm onto needles. Cast on 3 sts, work middle finger as Chart C, picking up 3 sts from the stitches cast on for ring finger, and working palm stitches as established. Work finger as charted. Finish the tip by cutting the yarn and threading it onto the tapestry needle. Then weave it through the remaining stitches and pull tight.

Pointer Finger
Slip pointer finger stitches from hand back onto needles and work as Chart C - Pointers & Pinkies (line up the side pattern in the chart with that already established), picking up 3 sts from those cast on between for the Middle finger. Work pointer finger as charted. Finish the tip by cutting the yarn and threading it onto the tapestry needle. Then weave it through the remaining stitches and pull tight.

Thumb
With palm up and fingertip facing you, pick up 17 sts from the stitches you cast on earlier. Pick up 1 st from side of thumb hole. Slip stitches from waste yarn onto needles. Pick up 1 st from side of thumb hole — 36 sts. Work thumb as charted, using Thumb for the outside of the thumb, and continuing the palm pattern for the inside of the thumb. Finish the tip by cutting the yarn and threading it onto the tapestry needle. Then weave it through the remaining stitches and pull tight.

Finishing
Weave in ends on wrong side. If a small hole shows at the base of the thumb or fingers, sew it closed using the yarn tail. Wash and block as desired.

Original gloves, Annemor Sundbø Collection

Chart D

Chart C

Chart C - Pointers & Pinkies

Chart A

Chart B

Annemor #13

Source
Annemor Sundbø
Private Collection

Finished Size
Women's Large to Men's Medium
Length: 10.5" from cuff to fingertip
Width: 4.5" measured across palm

Yarn
Harrisville New England Knitter's Shetland
(100% wool, 50g 197yd),
MC: 50 Black, 2 skeins – CC: 08 Hemlock, 1 skein

Gauge
32 sts and 33 rounds = 4"/10cm measured over palm

Needles & Notions
US Size 2 (2.75mm) DPN needles or size to give gauge
Waste Yarn, Tapestry Needle

MOST SELBUVOTTER WERE KNIT WITH A LIGHT BACKGROUND AND DARK PATTERN, BUT A REVERSED COLORWAY WAS ALSO POPULAR. THESE BEAUTIFUL REVERSED MITTENS FEATURE A LOVELY LILY AND VERY UNUSUAL HARP OR LYRE SHAPED PATTERN ON THE HAND BACK AND THUMB. THE ORIGINAL WAS SIZED FOR A WOMAN'S HAND, BUT WITH THE USE OF A RIBBED- AND STRANDED CUFF, IT'S HARD TO KNOW WHO WORE THEM. I THINK THEY'D MAKE A LOVELY GIFT FOR A HOLIDAY EXCHANGE, ESPECIALLY IF YOU DON'T KNOW WHO THE RECIPIENT WILL BE.
SAMPLE KNIT BY KIM MYHRE.

Cuff
Using MC, cast on 54 sts. Divide stitches evenly onto 4 needles and join circularly, taking care not to twist stitches. Work in K1P1 ribbing as follows:

1 Round MC
3 Rounds CC
1 Round MC
2 Rounds CC
4 Rounds MC

Knit 3 Rounds in MC, 2 Rounds in CC. Next Round increase as follows: *k5, M1; repeat 8 more times, k4 — 63 sts. Knit 1 more Round in MC. Work Chart A. Knit 2 Rounds in MC, 2 Rounds in CC, 3 more Rounds MC.

Lower Hand and Thumb Gusset
Begin Chart B, noting that charts are given for both Right and Left hands. Be sure to work one palm and the back for each mitten; if the "other" palm gets distracting, try photocopying the page and folding over the side not in use. Work the lower hand and thumb gusset, increasing stitches as charted — 75 sts.

Set Aside Thumb

On the next Round, knit as charted until you reach the thumb, which is represented in the chart by the grey bar. Slip the 15 thumb stitches onto waste yarn and cast on 15 sts using a backward loop method. Work the rest of the chart, and finish the fingertip by cutting the yarn and threading it onto the tapestry needle. Then thread through the remaining stitches and pull tight.

Thumb

With palm up and fingertip facing you, pick up 15 sts from the stitches you cast on earlier. Pick up 1 st from side of thumb hole. Slip stitches from waste yarn onto needles. Pick up 2 sts from side of thumb hole — 33 sts. Work thumb as charted, using Chart C for the outside of the thumb, and continuing the palm pattern for the inside of the thumb. Finish the thumb tip by cutting the yarn and threading it onto the tapestry needle. Then weave it through the remaining stitches and pull tight.

Finishing

Weave in ends on wrong side. If a small hole shows where the thumb was picked up, sew it closed using the yarn tail. Wash and block as desired.

Original mittens, Annemor Sundbø Collection

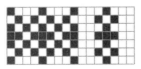

Chart A

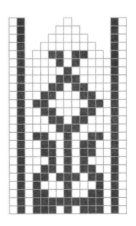

Chart C

Chart B

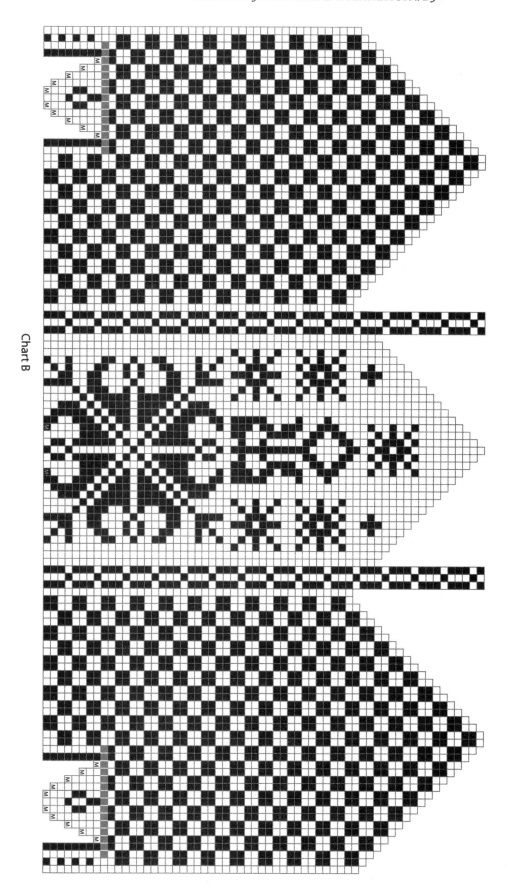

Annemor #14

Source
Annemor Sundbø
Private Collection

Finished Size
Girl's Large or Women's Small
Length: 9.25" from cuff to fingertip
Width: 4.25" measured across palm

Yarn
GGH Wollywasch (100% wool, 50g 137yd)
MC: 78 Blue, 1 skein
CC: 7 Brown, 1 skein

Gauge
33 sts and 34 rounds = 4"/10cm measured over palm

Needles & Notions
US Size 2 (2.75mm) DPN needles or size to give gauge
Waste Yarn, Tapestry Needle

ESTHER MUST HAVE LOVED HER MITTENS DEARLY, BECAUSE THE PALM IS SO WORN THAT IT WAS ENTIRELY COVERED WITH A KNITTED PATCH. I RECONSTRUCTED THE PALM WITH A SIMPLE FLORAL-INSPIRED PATTERN TO ECHO THE LARGE FLOWER ON THE BACK. THESE ALSO FEATURE AN UNUSUAL TWISTED RIB AT THE WRIST WHICH WILL PROVIDE A FIRM FIT, PERFECT FOR SKIING OR SNOWBALL FIGHTS. I USED A SUPERWASH YARN FROM THE BOTTOM OF MY STASH BASKET; SELBUVOTTER CAN BE MADE FROM ANY WOOL YARN.

Stitch Patterns
Twisted Rib (multiple of 4 + 2)
Round 1: Knit through back loop for 2 sts, Purl 2; repeat to end.

Cuff
Using MC, cast on 48 sts. Divide stitches evenly onto 4 needles and join circularly, taking care not to twist stitches. Work in Twisted Rib for 18 Rounds. Knit 1 Round. Next Round increase as follows: *k4, M1; repeat to end of Round — 60 sts. Knit 1 Round.

Lower Hand and Thumb Gusset
Begin Chart A, noting that charts are given for both Right and Left hands. Be sure to work one palm and the back for each mitten; if the "other" palm gets distracting, try photocopying the page and folding over the side not in use. Work the lower hand and thumb gusset, increasing stitches as charted — 72 sts.

Set Aside Thumb
On the next Round, knit as charted until you reach the thumb, which is represented in the chart by the grey bar. Slip the 17 thumb stitches onto waste yarn and cast on 17 sts using a backward loop method. Work the rest of the

chart, and finish the fingertip by cutting the yarn and threading it onto the tapestry needle. Then thread through the remaining stitches and pull tight.

Thumb

With palm up and fingertip facing you, pick up 17 sts from the stitches you cast on earlier. Pick up 1 st from side of thumb hole. Slip sts from waste yarn onto needles. Pick up 1 st from side of thumb hole — 36 sts. Work thumb as charted, using Chart B for the outside of the thumb, and continuing the palm pattern for the inside of the thumb. Finish the thumb tip by cutting the yarn and threading it onto the tapestry needle. Then weave it through the remaining stitches and pull tight.

Finishing

Weave in ends on wrong side. If a small hole shows where the thumb was picked up, sew it closed using the yarn tail. Wash and block as desired.

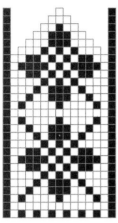

Chart B

Original mittens, Annemor Sundbø Collection

Chart A

Annemor #15

Source
Annemor Sundbø
Private Collection

Finished Size
Women's Medium or Men's Small
Length: 10.0" from cuff to fingertip
Width: 3.5" measured across palm

Yarn
Raumagarn Gammelserie (100% wool 50g 160m)
MC: 401 Ecru, 1 skein
CC: 436 Black, 1 skein

Gauge
30 sts and 31 rounds = 4"/10cm measured over palm

Needles & Notions
US Size 2 (2.75mm) DPN needles or size to give gauge
Waste Yarn, Tapestry Needle

THIS IS ANOTHER ONE OF MY FAVORITE PATTERNS, ALSO SHOWING A LILY DESIGN ON THE HAND. NOTICE THAT THE PINKY FINGER HAS A DIFFERENT PATTERN THAN THE OTHER FINGERS; I HAVEN'T SEEN ANOTHER PAIR LIKE THIS. WE HAVE NO WAY OF KNOWING IF THIS WAS SIGNIFICANT TO THE KNITTER OR JUST A MISTAKE THAT BECAME A DESIGN FEATURE. THE PINKY FINGER IS RATHER LONG; FEEL FREE TO SHORTEN IT WHEN YOU KNIT. I ESPECIALLY LIKE THIS UNUSUAL CUFF PATTERN AND PLAN TO USE IT IN OTHER PROJECTS.

Cuff
Using MC, cast on 56 sts. Divide stitches evenly onto 4 needles. Join circularly, taking care not to twist stitches. Work in K1P1 ribbing for 3 Rounds. Knit 1 Round in MC. Work Chart A. Knit 2 Round in MC, increasing on the first Round thusly: *k8, M1; repeat 7 times — 63 sts.

Lower Hand and Thumb Gusset
Begin Chart B, noting that charts are given for both Right and Left hands. Work the lower hand and thumb gusset, increasing stitches as charted — 73 sts.

Set Aside Thumb
On the next Round, knit as charted until you reach the thumb, which is represented in the chart by the grey bar. Slip the 15 thumb stitches onto waste yarn and cast on 14 sts using a backward loop method. Work the rest of Chart B.

Divide for Fingers
Notice the barred line at the top of Chart B. These lines show which stitches will be used for each finger. Work the back of the hand stitches in MC. Work across the pinky fingers on the palm. Slip the stitches for all stitches except the pinky finger onto waste yarn.

Pinky

Slip the pinky stitches onto 4 needles. Cast on 3 sts after the charted stitches on the back of the hand, then join the pinky finger into a Round — 20 sts. You will now knit only on the pinky stitches, beginning with the first row of Chart C. Work palm side as established. Finish the tip by cutting the yarn and threading it onto the tapestry needle. Then weave it through the remaining stitches and pull tight.

Ring Finger

Slip ring finger stitches onto needles. Beginning with hand back facing you, cast on 3 sts. Work across Chart C, pick up 3 sts from pinky cast-on stitches, work across palm. Continue working ring finger as charted. Finish the tip by cutting the yarn and threading it onto the tapestry needle. Then weave it through the remaining stitches and pull tight.

Middle Finger

Slip stitches from back and palm onto needles. Cast on 3 sts, work middle finger as Chart C, picking up 3 sts from the stitches cast on for ring finger, and working palm stitches as established. Work finger as charted. Finish the tip by cutting the yarn and threading it onto the tapestry needle. Then weave it through the remaining stitches and pull tight.

Pointer Finger

Slip pointer finger stitches from hand back onto needles and work as Chart C (line up the side pattern in the chart with that already established), picking up 3 sts from those cast on between for the middle finger. Work pointer finger as charted. Finish the tip by cutting the yarn and threading it onto the tapestry needle. Then weave it through the remaining stitches and pull tight.

Thumb

With palm up and fingertip facing you, pick up 14 sts from the stitches you cast on earlier. Pick up 1 st from side of thumb hole using CC. Slip stitches from waste yarn onto needles. Pick up 1 st from side of thumb hole using CC — 31 sts. The CC stitches picked up from the side of the thumb hole will become the outside stripe. Work thumb as charted, using Chart D for the outside of the thumb, and continuing the palm pattern for the inside of the thumb. Finish the tip by cutting the yarn and threading it onto the tapestry needle. Then weave it through the remaining stitches and pull tight.

Finishing

Weave in ends on wrong side. If a small hole shows at the base of the thumb or fingers, sew it closed using the yarn tail. Wash and block as desired.

Original gloves, Annemor Sundbø Collection

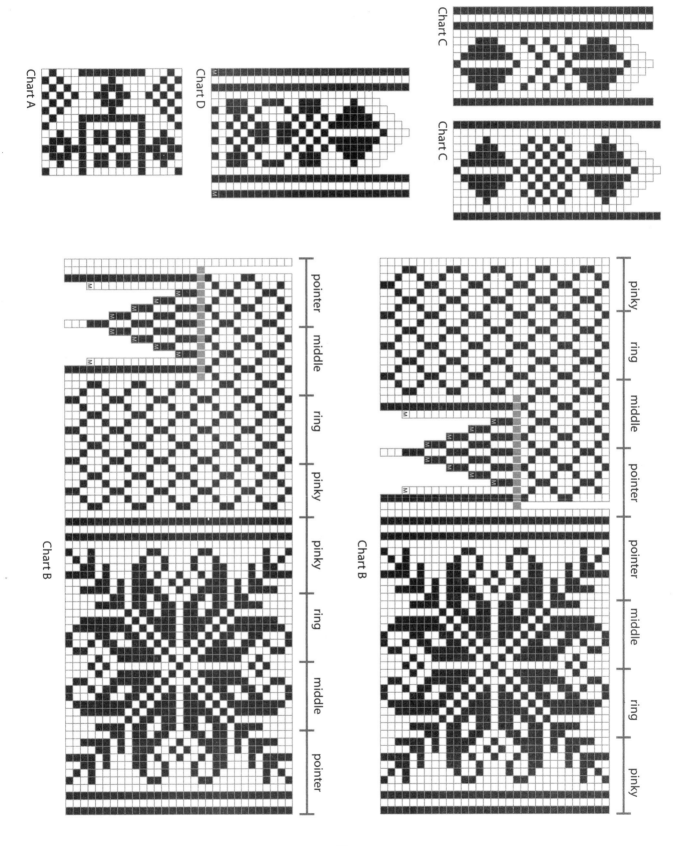

Annemor #16

Source
Annemor Sundbø
Private Collection

Finished Size
Women's Small/Medium
Length: 10.0" from cuff to fingertip
Width: 3.5" measured across palm

Yarn
Vuorelma Satakieli (100% wool, 25g 105m)
MC: 003 Ecru, 1 skein
CC: 696 Navy, 1 skein

Gauge
28 sts and 32 rounds = 4"/10cm measured over palm

Needles & Notions
US Size 2 (2.75mm) DPN needles or size to give gauge
Waste Yarn, Tapestry Needle

THESE MITTENS ARE CLASSIC MID-CENTURY SELBU, WITH THE DOUBLE STARS AND WONDERFUL USE OF FILLER PATTERNS. THEY USE MY FAVORITE PALM PATTERN; I'M THINKING OF USING IT ON A VEST. THE FIGURES ON THE CUFF LOOK LIKE ANCHORS. THE THUMB PATTERN IS ALSO QUITE UNUSUAL; THE KNITTER USED HALF-FIGURES TO FILL IN THE EMPTY SPACES LEFT BETWEEN THE MAIN STARS. THESE SAMPLES CAME OUT WOMEN'S SIZED, BUT YOU COULD KNIT THEM IN SPORT OR DK WEIGHT FOR A MAN'S SIZE. SAMPLE KNIT BY ELKA PRIEST.

Cuff
Using MC, cast on 60 sts. Divide stitches evenly onto 4 needles and join circularly, taking care not to twist stitches. Work in K2P1 ribbing for 4 Rounds. Knit 1 Round. Work Chart A. Knit 1 Round in MC.

Lower Hand and Thumb Gusset
Begin Chart B, noting that charts are given for both Right and Left hands. Be sure to work one palm and the back for each mitten; if the "other" palm gets distracting, try photocopying the page and folding over the side not in use. Work the lower hand and thumb gusset, increasing stitches as charted — 72 sts.

Set Aside Thumb
On the next Round, knit as charted until you reach the thumb, which is represented in the chart by the grey bar. Slip the 17 thumb stitches onto waste yarn and cast on 17 sts using a backward loop method. Work the rest of the chart, and finish the fingertip

Original mittens, Annemor Sundbø Collection

by cutting the yarn and threading it onto the tapestry needle. Then thread through the remaining stitches and pull tight.

Thumb

With palm up and fingertip facing you, pick up 17 sts from the stitches you cast on earlier. Pick up 1 st from side of thumb hole. Slip stitches from waste yarn onto needles. Pick up 1 st from side of thumb hole — 36 sts. Work thumb as charted, using Chart C for the outside of the thumb, and continuing the palm pattern for the inside of the thumb. Finish the thumb tip by cutting the yarn and threading it onto the tapestry needle. Then weave it through the remaining stitches and pull tight.

Finishing

Weave in ends on wrong side. If a small hole shows where the thumb was picked up, sew it closed using the yarn tail. Wash and block as desired.

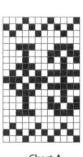

Chart A

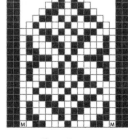

Chart C

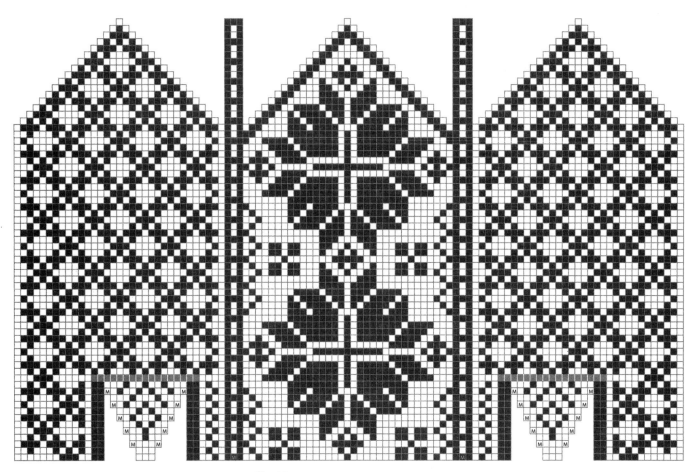

Chart B

Annemor #17

Source
Annemor Sundbø
Private Collection

Finished Size
Women's Large or Men's Small
Length: 10.0" from cuff to fingertip
Width: 3.5" measured across palm

Yarn
Raumagarn Gammelserie (100% wool 50g 160m)
MC: 401 Ecru, 1 skein
CC: 436 Black, 1 skein

Gauge
30 sts and 31 rounds = 4"/10cm measured over palm

Needles & Notions
US Size 2 (2.75mm) DPN needles or size to give gauge
Waste Yarn, Tapestry Needle

THIS BEAUTIFUL DESIGN WOULD MAKE AN EXCELLENT FIRST SELBU GLOVE PROJECT. USING THE SAME PATTERN FOR THE FINGERS AND THUMB SIMPLIFIES THINGS FOR THE KNITTER, AND THE SELBUROSE IS MORPHED INTO A STYLIZED SNOWFLAKE, WITH LIMITED STRETCHES OF A SINGLE COLOR. THAT MEANS NO LONG FLOATS TO WORRY ABOUT. FEEL FREE TO MODIFY THE FINGER AND THUMB LENGTHS TO SUIT THE WEARER. SAMPLE KNIT BY MARY SCHMELZER.

Cuff

Using MC, cast on 56 sts. Divide stitches evenly onto 4 needles. Join circularly, taking care not to twist stitches. Work Ribbing thusly: K2P1 to last 2 st, K1, P1. Work this for 3 Rounds. Work Chart A, Chart B, and Chart A again. Knit 2 Round in MC, increasing on the second Round as follows: *k8, M1; repeat to end — 63 Sts.

Lower Hand and Thumb Gusset

Begin Chart C, noting that charts are given for both Right and Left hands. Be sure to work one palm and the back for each mitten; if the "other" palm gets distracting, try photocopying the page and folding over the side not in use. Work the lower hand and thumb gusset, increasing stitches as charted — 73 sts.

Set Aside Thumb

On the next Round, knit as charted until you reach the thumb, which is represented in the chart by the grey bar. Slip the 15 thumb stitches onto waste yarn and cast on 14 sts using a backward loop method. Work the rest of Chart C.

Divide for Fingers

Notice the barred line at the top of Chart C. These lines show which stitches will be used for each finger. Work the back of the hand stitches in MC. Work across the pinky fingers on the palm. Slip the stitches for all stitches except the pinky finger onto waste yarn.

Pinky

Slip the pinky stitches onto 4 needles. Cast on 4 sts after the charted stitches on the back of the hand, then join the pinky finger into a Round. You will now knit only on the pinky stitches, beginning with the first row of Chart D. Work palm side as established. Finish the tip by cutting the yarn and threading it onto the tapestry needle. Then weave it through the remaining stitches and pull tight.

Ring Finger

Slip ring finger stitches onto needles. Beginning with hand back facing you, cast on 3 sts. Work across Chart E, pick up 4 sts from pinky cast-on stitches, work across palm. Continue working ring finger as charted. Finish the tip by cutting the yarn and threading it onto the tapestry needle. Then weave it through the remaining stitches and pull tight.

Middle Finger

Slip stitches from back and palm onto needles. Cast on 3 sts, work middle finger as Chart E, picking up 3 sts from the stitches cast on for ring finger, and working palm stitches as established. Work finger as charted. Finish the tip by cutting the yarn and threading it onto the tapestry needle. Then weave it through the remaining stitches and pull tight.

Pointer Finger

Slip pointer finger stitches from hand back onto needles and work as Chart E (line up the side pattern in the chart with that already established), picking up 3 sts from those cast on between for the Middle finger, and join in a Round. Work pointer finger as charted. Finish the tip by cutting the yarn and threading it onto

the tapestry needle. Then weave it through the remaining stitches and pull tight.

Thumb

With palm up and fingertip facing you, pick up 14 sts from the stitches you cast on earlier. Pick up 1 st from side of thumb hole. Slip stitches from waste yarn onto needles. Pick up 1 st from side of thumb hole — 31 sts. Work thumb as charted, using Chart E for the outside of the thumb, and continuing the palm pattern for the inside of the thumb. Finish the tip by cutting the yarn and threading it onto the tapestry needle. Then weave it through the remaining stitches and pull tight.

Finishing

Weave in ends on wrong side. If a small hole shows at the base of the thumb or fingers, sew it closed using the yarn tail. Wash and block as desired.

Original gloves, Annemor Sundbø Collection

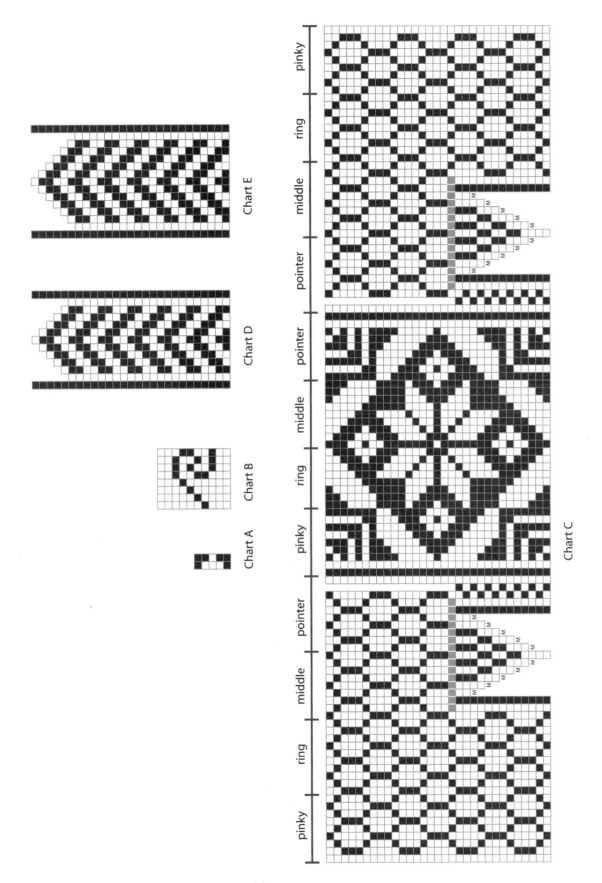

Chart E

Chart D

Chart B

Chart A

Chart C

Nhm #1

Source
Nordic Heritage Museum, Seattle WA
Accession Number 82.067.005

Finished Size
Women's Medium
Length: 9.5" from cuff to fingertip
Width: 3.75" measured across palm

Yarn
Jamieson & Smith jumper weight (100% wool, 25g 105m)
MC: 1A Ecru, 1 skein
CC: 80 Dark Brown, 1 skein

Gauge
32 sts and 32 rounds = 4"/10cm measured over palm

Needles & Notions
US Size 2 (2.75mm) DPN needles or size to give gauge
Waste Yarn, Tapestry Needle

No amount of yarn is too small to be used in a pair of mittens. The knitter who made these used three different shades of brown for the pattern color. I suspect the two mittens were worked at the same time to use up small balls of left overs ; the color changes happen on the same row on each hand. Use one color if you like, or use up those last little balls from other projects.

Cuff

Using MC, cast on 48 sts. Divide stitches evenly onto 4 needles and join circularly, taking care not to twist stitches. Work in K2P2 ribbing as follows:

10 Rounds MC
1 Round CC
1 Round MC
1 Round CC
1 Round MC
1 Round CC
8 Rounds MC.

Next Round in MC, increase as follows: *k8, M1; repeat to end of Round. 54 sts. Knit 4 Rounds in MC.

Lower Hand and Thumb Gusset

Begin Chart A, noting that charts are given for both Right and Left hands. Be sure to work one palm and the back for each mitten; if the "other" palm gets distracting, try photocopying the page and folding over the side not in use. Work the lower hand and thumb gusset, increasing stitches as charted — 60 sts.

Set Aside Thumb

On the next Round, knit as charted until you reach the thumb, which is represented in the chart by the grey bar. Slip the 11 thumb stitches onto waste yarn and cast on 11 sts using a backward loop method. Work the rest of the chart, and finish the fingertip by cutting the yarn and threading it onto the tapestry needle. Then thread through the remaining stitches and pull tight.

Thumb

With palm up and fingertip facing you, pick up 11 sts from the stitches you cast on earlier. Pick up 1 st from side of thumb hole. Slip stitches from waste yarn onto needles. Pick up 1 st from side of thumb hole — 24 sts. Work thumb as charted, using Chart B for the outside of the thumb, and continuing the palm pattern for the inside of the thumb. Finish the thumb tip by cutting the yarn and threading it onto the tapestry needle. Then weave it through the remaining stitches and pull tight.

Finishing

Weave in ends on wrong side. If a small hole shows where the thumb was picked up, sew it closed using the yarn tail. Wash and block as desired.

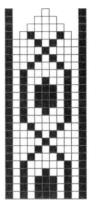

Chart B

Chart A

NHM #2

Source
Nordic Heritage Museum, Seattle WA
Accession Number 82.067.006

Finished Size
Girl's Large or Women's Small
Length: 14.25" from cuff to fingertip
Width: 3.25 measured across palm

Yarn
Jamieson & Smith jumper weight (100% wool, 25g 105m)
MC: 1A Ecru, 2 skeins
CC: 54 Grey, 1 skein

Gauge
36 sts and 32 rounds = 4"/10cm measured over palm

Needles & Notions
US Size 2 (2.75mm) DPN needles or size to give gauge
US Size 1/2.25 DPN needles
Waste Yarn, Tapestry Needle

THESE ARE THE ONLY MITTENS WITH THE BEAUTIFUL LONG GAUNTLET CUFF THAT I WAS ABLE TO REPRODUCE. UTTERLY FEMININE, AND SIZED FOR A GIRL'S HAND, THESE MITTENS WOULD BE STUNNING WHEN WORN WITH A FOLK COSTUME OR BUNAD, PERHAPS TUCKED INTO THE BELT FOR A 17 MAI CELEBRATION. THEY TAKE LONGER TO MAKE, DUE TO THE VERY LONG CUFF, SO BE SURE TO START WELL BEFORE SPRING. THE DISTINCTIVE BELL CURVE OF THE CUFF IS ACHIEVED THROUGH BLOCKING.
SAMPLE KNIT BY ANNE TURNER.

Cuff

Using smaller needles and MC, cast on 60 over 2 needles. Divide stitches evenly onto 4 needles and join circularly, taking care not to twist stitches. Knit 6 Rounds. Next Round work as follows: *k2tog, yo; repeat to end. Change to larger needles and knit 6 Rounds. Next Round, fold the hem to the inside (purl sides facing each other) and pick up stitch through the stitch on the needle AND through the cast on stitch rows below it. Pull new stitch through both to join the edge to the work. Knit 6 Rounds more then work Chart A. Knit 2 Rounds. Next Round, decrease as follows: *k3, k2tog; repeat to end of Round — 48 sts. Knit 2 Rounds. Work Chart B. Knit 2 Rounds MC.

Lower Hand and Thumb Gusset

Begin Chart C, noting that charts are given for both Right and Left hands. Be sure to work one palm and the back for each mitten; if the "other" palm gets distracting, try photocopying the page and folding over the side not in use. Work the lower hand and thumb gusset, increasing 6 sts as charted — 59 sts.

Set Aside Thumb

On the next Round, knit as charted until you

reach the thumb, which is represented in the chart by the grey bar. Slip the 11 thumb stitches onto waste yarn and cast on 10 sts using a backward loop method. Work the rest of the chart, and finish the fingertip by cutting the yarn and threading it onto the tapestry needle. Then thread through the remaining stitches and pull tight.

Thumb

With palm up and fingertip facing you, pick up 10 sts from the stitches you cast on earlier. Pick up 1 st from side of thumb hole. Slip stitches from waste yarn onto needles. Pick up 1 st from side of thumb hole — 23 sts. Work thumb as shown in Chart D. Finish the thumb tip by cutting the yarn and threading it onto the tapestry needle. Then weave it through the remaining stitches and pull tight.

Finishing

Weave in ends on wrong side. If a small hole shows where the thumb was picked up, sew it closed using the yarn tail. Wash and block as desired.

Original mittens
Nordic Heritage Museum, Seattle, WA
Accession Number 82.067.006

Chart B

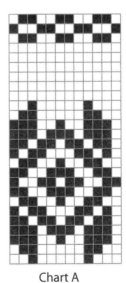

Chart A

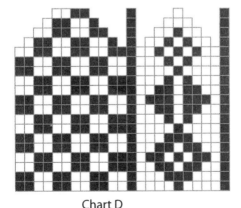

Chart D

Chart C

Nhm #3

Source
Nordic Heritage Museum, Seattle WA
Accession Number 83.030.004

Finished Size
Women's Small to Medium
Length: 9.5" from cuff to palm
Width: 3.75" measured across palm

Yarn
Jamieson & Smith jumper weight (100% wool, 25g 105m)
MC: 202 Beige, 2 skeins
CC: FC49 Blue, 1 skein

Gauge
34 sts and 33 rounds = 4"/10cm measured over palm

Needles & Notions
US Size 2 (2.75mm) DPN needles or size to give gauge
Waste Yarn, Tapestry Needle

THESE MITTENS CAME TO THE MUSEUM IN 1983 FROM A NORWEGIAN-NAMED DONOR, WITH NO INFORMATION BEYOND THE OBVIOUS "WOOL MITTENS KNIT IN BROWN AND GRAY." I WOULD GUESS THAT THEY WERE MADE BY AN IMMIGRANT OR FIRST GENERATION AMERICAN, SOME TIME IN THE MID TO LATE TWENTIETH CENTURY. WHITE AND BLACK MAY BE THE MOST COMMON COLORS FOR SELBUVOTTER, BUT YOU CAN USE ANY COLORS YOU LIKE SO LONG AS YOU'VE GOT A GOOD CONTRAST. IF I WERE TO KNIT THESE AGAIN, I WOULD USE A DARKER SHADE FOR THE PATTERN.

Cuff
Using MC, cast on 48 sts. Divide stitches evenly onto 4 needles and join circularly, taking care not to twist stitches. Work in K2P2 ribbing as follows:

8 Rounds MC
2 Rounds CC
2 Rounds MC
3 Rounds CC
2 Rounds MC
2 Rounds CC
6 Rounds MC.

Original mittens
Nordic Heritage Museum , Seattle, WA
Accession Number 83.030.004

Next Round increase as follows: *k4, M1; repeat to end of Round — 60 sts. Work Chart A.

Lower Hand and Thumb Gusset
Begin Chart B, noting that charts are given for both Right and Left hands. Be sure to work one palm and the back for each mitten; if the "other" palm gets distracting, try photocopying the page and folding over the side not in use. Work the lower hand and thumb gusset, increasing stitches as charted — 68 sts.

Set Aside Thumb

On the next Round, knit as charted until you reach the thumb, which is represented in the chart by the grey bar. Slip the 17 thumb stitches onto waste yarn and cast on 17 sts using a backward loop method. Work the rest of the chart, and finish the fingertip by cutting the yarn and threading it onto the tapestry needle. Then thread through the remaining stitches and pull tight.

Thumb

With palm up and fingertip facing you, pick up 17 sts from the stitches you cast on earlier. Pick up 1 st from side of thumb hole. Slip stitches from waste yarn onto needles. Pick up 1 st from side of thumb hole — 36 sts. Work thumb as charted, using Chart C for the outside of the thumb, and continuing the palm pattern for the inside of the thumb. Finish the thumb tip by cutting the yarn and threading it onto the tapestry needle. Then weave it through the remaining stitches and pull tight.

Finishing

Weave in ends on wrong side. If a small hole shows where the thumb was picked up, sew it closed using the yarn tail. Wash and block as desired.

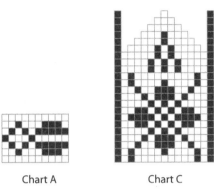

Chart A   Chart C

Chart B

Nhm #4

Source
Nordic Heritage Museum, Seattle WA
Accession Number 83.030.005

Finished Size
Women's Medium
Length: 12" from cuff to fingertip
Width: 4.25" measured across palm

Yarn
Jamieson & Smith jumper weight (100% wool, 25g 105m)
MC: 1A Ecru, 2 skein
CC: 80 Dark Brown, 1 skein

Gauge
38 sts and 36 rounds = 4"/10cm measured over palm

Needles & Notions
US Size 1.5 (2.25mm) DPN needles or size to give gauge
Waste Yarn, Tapestry Needle

WHEN I WAS SELECTING SAMPLES TO INCLUDE IN MY STUDY I NEARLY PASSED THESE OVER. THE PATTERN ON THE BACK IS DIFFERENT THAN THE OTHERS, SO I ASSUMED THAT THEY MUST HAVE ORIGINATED IN ANOTHER AREA OF NORWAY. I WAS INCORRECT, OF COURSE; THE CLOSER I LOOKED THROUGH SELBU DOCUMENTATION, THE MORE OFTEN I SAW THIS PATTERN. MOST SELBU MITTENS EMPLOY DECREASES THAT LEAN TOWARD THE CENTER OF THE HAND, AND AWAY FROM THE SIDE PATTERN. THESE MITTENS DO THE OPPOSITE. PAY CLOSE ATTENTION TO THE CHART, AND REFER TO THE PICTURE TO MAKE SURE YOU'RE DOING IT RIGHT.
SAMPLE KNIT BY MIRIAM FELTON.

Pattern

Seed Stitch (multiple of 2)
Round 1: *k1 p1; repeat from * to end of Round.
Round 2: *p1, k1; repeat from * to end of Round.

Repeat these two Rounds for pattern.

Twisted Rib (multiple of 2)
Round 1: *Knit 1 through back loop, p1; repeat from * to end of Round.

Repeat for pattern.

Cuff

Using MC, cast on 72 sts. Divide stitches evenly onto 4 needles and join circularly, taking care not to twist stitches. Work in Seed Stitch for 5 Rounds. Work in Twisted Rib as follows:

10 Rounds MC	1 Round CC
2 Rounds CC	2 Rounds MC
2 Rounds MC	2 Rounds CC
1 Round CC	8 Rounds MC.
1 Round MC	

Knit 1 Round in MC. Work Chart A. Knit 3 Rounds in MC, decreasing 2 sts on the 3rd

Round. Work Chart B. Knit 1 Round in MC, increasing 4 sts evenly around — 74 sts.

Lower Hand and Thumb

Begin Chart C, noting that charts are given for both Right and Left hands. Be sure to work one palm and the back for each mitten; if the "other" palm gets distracting, try photocopying the page and folding over the side not in use. Work as charted until you reach the thumb, which is represented in the chart by the grey bar. Slip the 15 thumb stitches onto waste yarn and cast on 15 sts using a backward loop method. Work the rest of the chart, and finish the fingertip by cutting the yarn and threading it onto the tapestry needle. Then thread through the remaining stitches and pull tight.

Thumb

With palm up and fingertip facing you, pick up 15 sts from the stitches you cast on earlier. Pick up 1 st from side of thumb hole. Slip stitches from waste yarn onto needles. Pick up 1 st from side of thumb hole — 32 sts. Next Round, decrease the stitches picked up from the side of the thumb hole — 30 sts. Work thumb as charted, using Chart D for the outside of the thumb, and continuing the palm pattern for the inside of the thumb. Finish the thumb tip by cutting the yarn and threading it onto the tapestry needle. Then weave it through the remaining stitches and pull tight.

Finishing

Weave in ends on wrong side. If a small hole shows where the thumb was picked up, sew it closed using the yarn tail. Wash and block as desired.

Original mittens
Nordic Heritage Museum , Seattle, WA
Accession Number 83.030.005

Chart B

Chart A

Chart D

Key

k2tog

SSK

Chart C

NHM #5

Source
Nordic Heritage Museum, Seattle WA
Accession Number 86.005.002

Finished Size
Toddler
Length: 7" from cuff to fingertip
Width: 3" measured across palm

Yarn
Dalegarn Baby Ull (100% wool, 50g 180m)
MC: 0010 White, 1 skein
CC: 9013 Green, 1 skein

Gauge
32 sts and 32 rounds = 4"/10cm measured over palm

Needles & Notions
US Size 2 (2.75mm) DPN needles or size to give gauge
Waste Yarn, Tapestry Needle

MY FIRST IMPRESSION OF THESE LITTLE MITTENS WAS MIXED; I LOVED THEIR BRIGHT RED COLOR, AND CLEAN DESIGN, BUT I COULDN'T UNDERSTAND WHY THE RIGHT HAND WAS TWISTED. HAD THE WEARER'S MOTHER BEEN CARELESS WHEN LEAVING THEM TO DRY? ON CLOSER INSPECTION I REALIZED THAT INSTEAD OF A RIGHT HAND MITTEN, IT WAS A LEFT MITTEN THAT HAD BEEN WORN ON THE RIGHT HAND. MOMMY HAD FINISHED THE PAIR, PERHAPS WITH LEFTOVER YARN FROM SOMEONE'S FAVORITE SWEATER, AND THEN REALIZED TOO LATE THAT SHE HAD MADE A MISTAKE. BUT WHEN THE SNOW IS FALLING, A CHILD REALLY WON'T WAIT FOR YOU TO KNIT A NEW ONE. SO IT'S TWO LEFT MITTENS, TWO WARM HANDS, AND A WONDERFUL MYSTERY FOR US TODAY.

Cuff

Using MC, cast on 36 sts. Divide stitches evenly onto 4 needles and join circularly, taking care not to twist stitches. Work in K2P2 ribbing as follows:

10 Rounds MC
1 Round CC
1 Round MC
1 Round CC
1 Round MC
1 Round CC
2 Rounds MC.

Original mittens
Nordic Heritage Museum , Seattle, WA
Accession Number 86.005.002

Next Round in MC, increase as follows: *k6, M1; repeat to end of Round — 42 sts. Knit 2 more Rounds in MC.

Lower Hand and Thumb Gusset

Begin Chart A, noting that charts are given for both Right and Left hands. Be sure to work one palm and the back for each mitten; if the "other" palm gets distracting, try photocopying the page and folding over the side not in use. Work the lower hand and thumb gusset, increasing stitches as charted — 48 sts.

Set Aside Thumb

On the next Round, knit as charted until
you reach the thumb, which is represented in
the chart by the grey bar. Slip the 9 thumb
stitches onto waste yarn and cast on 9 sts using
a backward loop method. Work the rest of the
chart, and finish the fingertip by cutting the yarn
and threading it onto the tapestry needle. Then
thread through the remaining stitches and pull
tight.

Thumb

With palm up and fingertip facing you, pick up 9
sts from the stitches you cast on earlier. Pick up
1 st from side of thumb hole. Slip stitches from
waste yarn onto needles. Pick up 1 st from side of
thumb hole — 20 sts. Work thumb as charted,
using Chart B for the outside of the thumb, and
continuing the palm pattern for the inside of the
thumb. Finish the thumb tip by cutting the yarn
and threading it onto the tapestry needle. Then
weave it through the remaining stitches and pull
tight.

Finishing

Weave in ends on wrong side. If a small hole
shows where the thumb was picked up, sew it
closed using the yarn tail. Wash and block as
desired.

Chart B

Chart A

$\mathcal{N}$HM #6

Source
Nordic Heritage Museum, Seattle WA
Accession Number 87.028.005

Finished Size
Women's Medium
Length: 11.25" from cuff to fingertip
Width: 3.25" measured across palm

Yarn
Hifa Kamgarn Tynt (100% wool, 200g 1400m)
MC: 897 Brown, 1 cone
CC: 826 Ecru, 1 cone

Gauge
25 sts and 25 rounds = **2"/5cm** measured over palm

Needles & Notions
US Size 00 (1.75mm) DPN needles or size to give gauge
Waste Yarn, Tapestry Needle

I READ SOMEWHERE, "NOTHING TRAVELS FASTER THAN A KNITTING PATTERN."
ALTHOUGH THESE MITTENS WERE KNIT IN ICELAND OR BY ICELANDIC IMMIGRANTS, THE DESIGN
PATTERNS ARE PURE SELBU. ICELANDIC MITTENS ARE TYPICALLY WORKED IN BANDS OF SIMPLE
PATTERNS, RATHER THAN A COMPLEX ALL-OVER, SO HERE THE KNITTER REINTERPRETED THE
SELBU DESIGNS INTO HER OWN TRADITIONS. THE MAIN PATTERN ON THE HAND BACK IS,
ONCE AGAIN, FOUND IN NORWEGIAN KNITTING DESIGN BY ANNICHEN SIBBERN BØHN,
AND SHE LABELS IT SPECIFICALLY AS A "MITTEN FROM SELBU." ANNEMOR SUNDBØ
IDENTIFIES THE PATTERN AS A SPIDER, SITTING IN A BOUGH OF PINE BRANCHES.
SAMPLE KNIT BY EYJA BRYNJARSDÓTTIR.

Cuff

Using MC, cast on 72 sts. Divide stitches evenly onto 4 needles and join circularly, taking care not to twist stitches. Work in K1P1 ribbing as follows:

10 Rounds MC	3 Rounds MC
2 Rounds CC	1 Round CC
4 Rounds MC	4 Rounds MC
1 Round CC	2 Rounds CC
3 Rounds	14 Rounds MC.
1 Round CC	

Knit 4 Rounds in MC, increasing every 9 sts on the first Round for 80 sts. Work Chart A. Knit 2 Rounds in MC.

Thumb

Right Hand: Knit 42, m1, Knit 14 sts with waste yarn. Slip the waste yarn stitches back to left needle and knit them with the MC yarn. M1, then complete Round (22 more stitches) — 82 sts.

Left Hand: Knit 64, m1, Knit 14 sts with waste yarn. Slip the waste yarn stitches back to left needle and knit them with the MC yarn. M1, then complete Round (2 more stitches) — 82 sts.

Both Hands: Knit 2 more Rounds in MC. Work Chart B. Finish fingertip using Kitchener Stitch, or turn mitten inside out and work 3-needle bind off.

Thumb

Slip thumb stitches off waste yarn and divide evenly onto needles, picking up one extra stitch from the sides of the holes. Work thumb in MC for 2" or desired length. K2tog all around until 8 sts remain. Break yarn and thread through remaining stitches and pull tight.

Finishing

Weave in ends on wrong side. If a small hole shows where the thumb was picked up, sew it closed using the yarn tail. Wash and block as desired.

Original mittens
Nordic Heritage Museum , Seattle, WA
Accession Number 87.028.005

This pattern proposed several challenges. First, the soft Icelandic *þel* yarn that was originally used is no longer commercially available. Eyja Brynjarsdottir, the talented knitter who made up these samples, tried several different Icelandic yarns but was unhappy with the results. We decided to try the Norwegian Hifa Kamgarn Tynt which I had on hand for another pair in the collection. The results speak for themselves. However, as a result of the difference in yarn gauges, the hands are much longer than the originals. Rather than redesign the pattern and reknit the sample, I suggest you shorten the cuff, move the thumb up the chart about an inch and a half, and work the pointed fingertip that Eyja has done instead of the flat, grafted one in the original. Or, reinterpret the design in your own yarn. This would be a wonderful project for a handspinner.

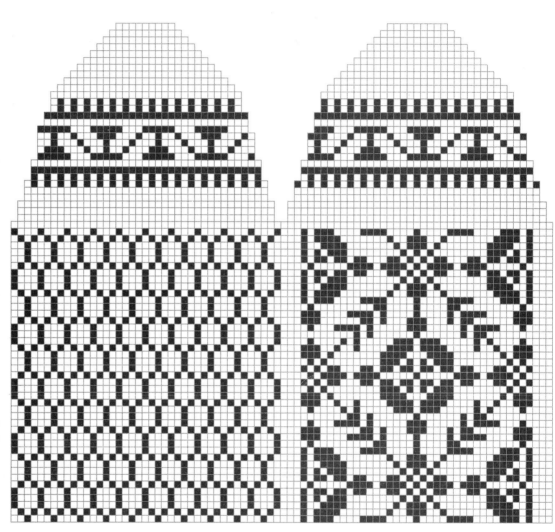

Chart B

put the thumb
somewhere around here

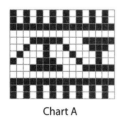

Chart A

ℕHM #7

Source
Nordic Heritage Museum, Seattle, WA
Accession Number 1995.049.015

Finished Size
Women's Medium
Length: 10.25" from cuff to fingertip
Width: 3.75" measured across palm

Yarn
Vuorelma Satakieli (100% wool, 25g 105m)
MC: Natural, 1 skein
CC: Dark Brown, 1 skein

Gauge
37 sts and 37 rounds = 4"/10cm measured over palm

Needles & Notions
US Size 1.5 (2.25mm) DPN needles or size to give gauge
Waste Yarn, Tapestry Needle

OF ALL THE MITTENS IN THE COLLECTION, THESE ARE THE ONES I LIKE FOR MYSELF. I FIND THE MAIN PATTERN SO ELEGANT, AND I LOVE THE LOOK OF A PATTERNED CUFF. THE MAIN PATTERN IS A STYLIZED LILY, ACCORDING TO ANNEMOR SUNDBØ, AND SYMBOLIZES PURITY AND THE VIRGIN MARY. LILIES ARRANGED IN A ROSETTE PATTERN AS SEEN HERE WERE OFTEN USED IN WOVEN TAPESTRIES IN THE COUNTY TRONDELAG, WHERE SELBU IS SITUATED. THE PALM PATTERN, REMINISCENT OF THE QUILTING PATTERN DOUBLE IRISH CHAIN, IS COMPLEX AND UNLESS THE KNITTER MEMORIZES THE RHYTHM OF EACH ROW, IT WILL BE DIFFICULT TO KNIT.

Cuff
Using MC, cast on 60 sts. Divide stitches evenly onto 4 needles and join circularly, taking care not to twist stitches. Work in K2P2 ribbing for 4 rounds. Work Chart A. Knit 4 Rounds in MC.

Lower Hand and Thumb Gusset
Begin Chart B, noting that charts are given for both Right and Left hands. Be sure to work one palm and the back for each mitten; if the "other" palm gets distracting, try photocopying the page and folding over the side not in use. Work the lower hand and thumb gusset, increasing stitches as charted — 74 sts.

Set Aside Thumb
On the next Round, knit as charted until you reach the thumb, which is represented in the chart by the grey bar. Slip the 15 thumb stitches onto waste yarn and cast on 12 sts using a backward loop method. Work the rest of the chart, and finish the fingertip by cutting the yarn and threading it onto the tapestry needle. Then thread through the remaining stitches and pull tight.

Thumb
With palm up and fingertip facing you, pick up 11 sts from the stitches you cast on earlier. Pick

up 1 st from side of thumb hole. Slip stitches from waste yarn onto needles. Pick up 1 st from side of thumb hole — 28 sts. Work thumb as charted, using Chart C for the outside of the thumb, and continuing the palm pattern for the inside of the thumb. Finish the thumb tip by cutting the yarn and threading it onto the tapestry needle. Then weave it through the remaining stitches and pull tight.

Finishing

Weave in ends on wrong side. If a small hole shows where the thumb was picked up, sew it closed using the yarn tail. Wash and block as desired.

Original mittens
Nordic Heritage Museum, Seattle WA
Accession Number 1995.049.015

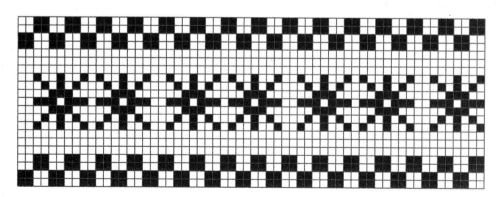

Chart A

Chart C

Chart B

NHM #8

Source
Nordic Heritage Museum, Seattle, WA
Accession Number 1995.061.001

Finished Size
Men's Medium or Large
Length: 10" from cuff to fingertip
Width: 5" wide across palm at knuckles

Yarn
Jamieson & Smith jumper weight (100% wool, 25g 105m)
MC: Shade 1A Ecru, 2 skeins
CC: Shade 4 Brown, 1 skein

Gauge
28 sts and 32 rounds = 4"/10cm measured over palm

Needles & Notions
US Size 2 (2.75mm) DPN needles or size to give gauge
Waste Yarn, Tapestry Needle

THESE MITTENS CAST A SPECIAL SPELL OVER ME. LIKE THE DARK BROWN PAIR FROM ICELAND, THEY FEATURE A PINE BOUGHS PATTERN ON THE BACK OF THE HAND, BUT HERE THE PALM IS WORKED IN TRIANGLES, SYMBOLS OF THE HOLY TRINITY. I'M NOT SURE IF THE MAGIC WAS THE DELICATE BRANCHES OF THE BACK OR THE CAREFULLY WOVEN HOLE ON THE HEEL OF THE HAND, OR POSSIBLY THE FACT THAT THE TWO HANDS USE DIFFERENT STAR PATTERNS ON THE CUFF. EITHER WAY, THESE ARE LOVELY TO KNIT AND TO WEAR.
SAMPLE KNIT BY JUDY SEIP.

Cuff
Using MC, cast on Cast on 56 sts. Divide evenly onto 4 needles and join circularly, taking care not to twist stitches. Work 1 Round K1P1 ribbing, one Round plain in MC. Work Chart A for the cuff.

Lower Hand
Begin Chart B, noting that charts are given for both Right and Left hands. Be sure to work one palm and the back for each mitten; if the "other" palm gets distracting, try photocopying the page and folding over the side not in use. Work the lower hand and thumb gusset, increasing 9 sts as charted — 65 sts.

Set Aside Thumb
On the next Round, knit as charted until you reach the thumb, which is represented in the chart by the grey bar. Slip the 13 thumb stitches onto waste yarn and cast on 15 sts in color as established. Then finish the row.

Palm and Fingers

Work the rest of the chart as established. Finish the fingertip by cutting the yarn and threading it onto the tapestry needle. Then thread through the remaining stitches and pull tight.

Thumb

Remove waste yarn and slip stitches all around the hole onto needles, picking up one extra stitch between the front and back — 32 sts. Begin thumb as shown in Chart C and the palm-side as established in palm pattern, decreasing over those picked up stitches — 30 sts. (This increase and then immediate decrease covers up the hole that invariably forms when adding the thumb.) Work back of thumb as shown in Chart B and palm-side of thumb as established for palm. Finish the thumb tip by cutting the yarn and threading it onto the tapestry needle. Then thread through the remaining stitches and pull tight.

Finishing

If holes remain on the side of the thumbs, where stitches were picked up, stitch them closed using the yarn tail or spare yarn. Weave in all ends and wash mittens to block.

Original mittens
Nordic Heritage Museum , Seattle WA
Accession Number 1995.061.001

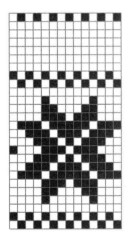

Chart A

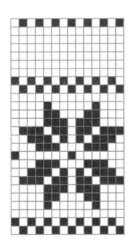

Chart A - another option

Chart C

Chart B

106

ℵHM #9

Source
Nordic Heritage Museum, Seattle WA
Accession Number 1995.061.002

Finished Size
Women's Medium
Length: 9.5" from cuff to fingertip
Width: 3.75" measured across palm

Yarn
Jamieson's Double Knitting (100% wool, 25g 175m)
MC: 104 Natural White, 2 skeins
CC: 235 Grouse, 2 skeins

Gauge
28 sts and 32 rounds = 4"/10cm measured over palm

Needles & Notions
US Size 2 (2.75mm) DPN needles or size to give gauge
US Size 1 (2.55mm) DPN needles
Waste Yarn, Tapestry Needle

I LOVE THE FLEXIBILITY THE SELBUVOTTER METHOD. THESE MITTENS WERE ORIGINALLY KNIT IN THE SMOOTH SELBUGARN WHICH IS NOW IMPOSSIBLE TO FIND. I PLANNED TO USE SATAKIELI AS A SUBSTITUTE, BUT ACCIDENTALLY SENT DENISE, MY TALENTED TEST KNITTER, THE WRONG YARN FOR THE CONTRASTING PATTERN COLOR. YIKES! DENISE GRACIOUSLY OFFERED TO USE SOME YARN FROM HER STASH, AND CHOSE SOMETHING I HADN'T THOUGHT OF - JAMIESON'S DOUBLE KNITTING. DENISE BEAUTIFULLY ILLUSTRATED HOW CHOOSING YOUR OWN YARNS CAN MAKE MITTENS THAT ARE UNIQUELY YOUR OWN. WHILE THE STRANDED CUFF IMPLIES THESE ARE A MAN'S MITTENS, THEY WORKED UP TO FIT MY HAND PERFECTLY.
SAMPLE KNIT BY DENISE SATTERLUND.

Cuff
Using MC and smaller needles, cast on 60 sts. Divide stitches evenly onto 4 needles and join circularly, taking care not to twist stitches. Work in K1P1 ribbing for 4 Rounds. Change to larger needles and work Chart A. Knit one Round in MC.

Lower Hand and Thumb Gusset
Begin Chart B, noting that charts are given for both Right and Left hands. Be sure to work one palm and the back for each mitten; if the "other" palm gets distracting, try photocopying the page and folding over the side not in use. Work the lower hand and thumb gusset, increasing stitches as charted — 66 sts.

Set Aside Thumb
On the next Round, knit as charted until you reach the thumb, which is represented in the chart by the grey bar. Slip the 15 thumb stitches onto waste yarn and cast on 13 sts using a

backward loop method. Work the rest of the chart, and finish the fingertip by cutting the yarn and threading it onto the tapestry needle. Then thread through the remaining stitches and pull tight.

Thumb

With palm up and fingertip facing you, pick up 13 sts from the stitches you cast on earlier. Pick up 1 st from side of thumb hole. Slip stitches from waste yarn onto needles. Pick up 1 st from side of thumb hole — 30 sts. Work thumb as charted, using Chart C for the outside of the thumb, and continuing the palm pattern for

the inside of the thumb. Finish the thumb tip by cutting the yarn and threading it onto the tapestry needle. Then weave it through the remaining stitches and pull tight.

Finishing

Weave in ends on wrong side. If a small hole shows where the thumb was picked up, sew it closed using the yarn tail. Wash and block as desired.

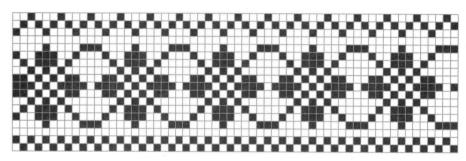

Chart A

Chart C

Original mittens
Nordic Heritage Museum, Seattle WA
Accession Number 1995.061.002

Chart B

NHM #10

Source
Nordic Heritage Museum, Seattle, WA
Accession Number 2002.134.001

Finished Size
Girls Large or Women's Small
Length: 10.0" from cuff to fingertip
Width: 3.5" measured across palm

Yarn
Hifa Kamgarn Tynt (100% wool, 200g 1400m)
MC: 826 Ecru, 1 cone
CC: 897 Brown, 1 cone

Gauge
38 sts and 38 rounds = 4"/10cm measured over palm

Needles & Notions
US Size 0 (2.00mm) DPN needles or size to give gauge
Waste Yarn, Tapestry Needle

I FEEL THESE ARE THE MOST BEAUTIFUL MITTENS IN THE COLLECTION. THE SCROLL APPEARS INSPIRED BY ROSMALING. THE PATTERNS ARE NOT SYMMETRICAL, EITHER ON THE SAME MITTEN OR BETWEEN THE TWO HANDS, WHICH MAKES ME THINK THEY WERE DESIGNED ON THE NEEDLE RATHER THAN CHARTED ON GRAPH PAPER BEFOREHAND. AFTER MANY PAINSTAKING HOURS OF TRYING TO CHART EVERY BEAUTIFUL, IMPERFECT STITCH (TWICE), JUST AS ORIGINALLY KNIT, I FINALLY CRIED UNCLE AND CREATED A SYMMETRICAL CHART. FEEL FREE TO MAKE A FEW MISTAKES IF YOU WANT TO MIMIC THE ORIGINALS. THE ORIGINAL MITTENS, KNIT AT 9 1/2 STITCHES PER INCH, AND WOULD FIT A LARGE MAN'S HAND. MIRIAM FELTON KNIT THE SAMPLES AT AN AMAZING 13 STITCHES PER INCH USING A YARN MOST WOULD CONSIDER LACE WEIGHT AND THEY FIT A SMALL WOMAN'S HAND.
SAMPLE KNIT BY MIRIAM FELTON.

Cuff
Using MC, cast on 76 sts. Divide stitches evenly onto 4 needles and join circularly, taking care not to twist stitches. Work in K1P1 ribbing for 2 Rounds.

Lower Hand and Thumb Gusset
Work Chart A. Work one Round plain in MC, increasing 2 sts evenly around. Begin Chart B, noting that charts are given for both Right and Left hands. Be sure to work one palm and the back for each mitten; if the "other" palm gets distracting, try photocopying the page and folding over the side not in use. Work the lower hand and thumb gusset, increasing stitches as charted — 91 sts.

Set Aside Thumb

On the next Round, knit as charted until you reach the thumb, which is represented in the chart by the grey bar. Slip the 17 thumb stitches onto waste yarn and cast on 10 sts using a backward loop method. Work the rest of the chart, and finish the fingertip by cutting the yarn and threading it onto the tapestry needle. Then thread through the remaining stitches and pull tight.

Thumb

With palm up and fingertip facing you, pick up 10 sts from the stitches you cast on earlier. Pick up 2 sts from side of thumb hole. Slip stitches from waste yarn onto needles. Pick up 2 sts from side of thumb hole — 31 sts. Work thumb as charted, using Chart C for the outside of the thumb, and continuing the palm pattern for the inside of the thumb. Finish the thumb tip by cutting the yarn and threading it onto the tapestry needle. Then weave it through the remaining stitches and pull tight.

Finishing

Weave in ends on wrong side. If a small hole shows where the thumb was picked up, sew it closed using the yarn tail. Wash and block as desired.

Original mittens
Nordic Heritage Museum , Seattle, WA
Accession Number 2002.134.001

Chart C

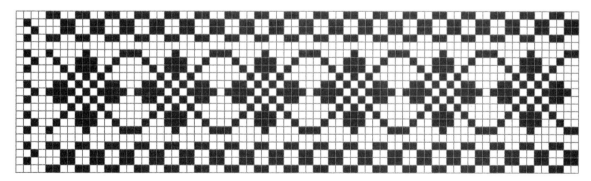

Chart A

Chart B

𝒩HM #11

Source
Nordic Heritage Museum, Seattle, WA
Accession Number 2006.008.001

Finished Size
Child Large to Adult S/M
Length: 9.5″ form cuff to fingertip
Width: 4″ measured across palm

Yarn
Dalegarn Heilo (100% wool, 50g, 109 yds)
MC: 0017 Natural White, 2 skeins
CC: 0090 Black, 1 skein

Gauge
26 st 28 rounds = 4″/10cm measured over palm

Needles & Notions
US Size 3 (3.0mm) DPN needles or size to give gauge
Waste Yarn, Tapestry Needle

THIS A MODERN PATTERN WITH UNISEX STYLING, WORKED WITH REINDEER IN A DK WEIGHT YARN; THEY'RE A GREAT FIRST SELBUVOTTER PATTERN. ORIGINALLY SIZED FOR A CHILD, THEY WORK UP ADULT SIZED IN TODAY'S YARN. NOTE HOW THE THUMB GUSSET CHECKERBOARD HAS BEEN MODIFIED TO FORM A HEART. THE RIBBED CUFF IS WORKED NARROW FOR A CHILD'S SIZED WRIST. FOR ADULT SIZE YOU MIGHT CONSIDER CASTING ON 48 STITCHES AND WORKING THE STRIPE PATTERN AS SHOWN, BUT DON'T INCREASE AFTER THE RIBBING. JUST WORK ONE MORE ROUND IN MC.

Cuff
Using MC, cast on 40 sts. Divide stitches evenly onto 4 needles and join circularly, taking care not to twist stitches. Work in K1P1 ribbing as follows:

4 Rounds MC
2 Rounds CC
4 Rounds MC
2 Rounds CC
4 Rounds MC
2 Rounds CC
4 Rounds MC.

Next Round in MC increase as follows: *k5, M1; repeat all around — 48 Sts. Knit 2 Rounds.

Lower Hand and Thumb Gusset
Work Chart A. Knit 2 Rounds in MC. Begin Chart B, noting that separate charts are given for both Right and Left hands. Work the lower hand and thumb gusset, increasing stitches as charted — 60 sts.

Set Aside Thumb
On the next Round, knit as charted until you reach the thumb, which is represented in the chart by the grey bar. Slip the 13 thumb stitches

onto waste yarn and cast on 13 sts using a backward loop method. Work the rest of the chart, and finish the fingertip by cutting the yarn and threading it onto the tapestry needle. Then thread through the remaining stitches and pull tight.

Thumb

With palm up and fingertip facing you, pick up 13 sts from the stitches you cast on earlier. Pick up 1 st from side of thumb hole. Slip stitches from waste yarn onto needles. Pick up 1 st from side of thumb hole — 28 sts. Work thumb as charted, using Chart C for the outside of the thumb, and continuing the palm pattern for the inside of the thumb. Finish the thumb tip by cutting the yarn and threading it onto the tapestry needle. Then weave it through the remaining stitches and pull tight.

Finishing

Weave in ends on wrong side. If a small hole shows where the thumb was picked up, sew it closed using the yarn tail. Wash and block as desired.

Chart B - Left Hand

Chart A   Chart C   Chart B - Right Hand

NHM #12

Source
Nordic Heritage Museum, Seattle, WA
Accession Number 2008.006.002

Finished Size
Adult Medium
Length: 11" from cuff to fingertip
Width: 4.25" measured across palm

Yarn
Dalegarn Heilo (100% wool, 50g, 109 yds)
MC: 0017 Natural White, 2 skeins
CC: 0090 Black, 1 skein

Gauge
28 sts and 28 rounds = 4"/10cm measured over palm

Needles & Notions
US Size 3 (3.00mm) DPN needles or size to give gauge
Waste Yarn, Tapestry Needle

THESE MITTEN WERE DESIGNED BY SOMEONE WHO KNEW WHAT SELBU MITTENS LOOK LIKE, BUT NOT WHY, NOR HOW THE CONSTRUCTION AND THE APPEARANCE ARE LINKED. THE LARGE STAR ON THE BACKS, WITH THEIR DELICATE OUTLINE, ARE UNUSUAL, BUT THE THUMB IS ALL WRONG. THE KNITTER CAST ON (NEARLY) ENOUGH STITCHES FOR THE WHOLE HAND AND FORCED THE SIGNATURE CHECKERBOARD ONTO A FLAT SPACE. THIS LEFT A GLARING BLANK WHITE SPACE AND A MESS WHERE THE CHECKERBOARD RAMMED INTO THE PALM PATTERN. THEN THE THUMB WAS WORKED AS A SIMPLE "PEASANT" THUMB, AND THE WHOLE REASON FOR THE CHECKERBOARD WAS LOST. STILL, THE MITTENS ARE BEAUTIFUL, AND IT WILL BE LEFT AS AN EXERCISE TO THE DEDICATED KNITTER TO MODIFY THE STITCH COUNT AND IMPLEMENT A PROPER GUSSET IF DESIRED.
KNIT THEM AS CHARTED FOR AN EASY PROJECT.

Cuff
Using MC, cast on 56 sts. Divide stitches evenly onto 4 needles and join circularly, taking care not to twist stitches. Work in K2P2 ribbing as follows:

8 Rounds MC
2 Rounds CC
2 Rounds MC
1 Round CC
1 Round MC

1 Round CC
1 Round MC
1 Round CC
2 Rounds MC
2 Rounds CC
6 Rounds MC

Work Chart A. Knit 2 Rounds in MC, increasing 4 sts evenly around on the first Round — 60 Sts.

Hand

Begin Chart B, noting that charts are given for both Right and Left hands. Be sure to work one palm and the back for each mitten; if the "other" palm gets distracting, try photocopying the page and folding over the side not in use.

Work as charted until you reach the thumb, which is represented in the chart by the grey bar. Slip the 13 thumb stitches onto waste yarn and cast on 13 sts using a backward loop method. Work the rest of the chart, and finish the fingertip by cutting the yarn and threading it onto the tapestry needle. Then thread through the remaining stitches and pull tight.

Thumb

With palm up and fingertip facing you, pick up 13 sts from the stitches you cast on earlier. Pick up 1 st from side of thumb hole. Slip stitches from waste yarn onto needles. Pick up 1 st from side of thumb hole — 28 sts. Work thumb as charted, using Chart C for the outside of the thumb, and continuing the palm pattern for the inside of the thumb. Finish the thumb tip by cutting the yarn and threading it onto the tapestry needle. Then weave it through the remaining stitches and pull tight.

Finishing

Weave in ends on wrong side. If a small hole shows where the thumb was picked up, sew it closed using the yarn tail. Wash and block as desired.

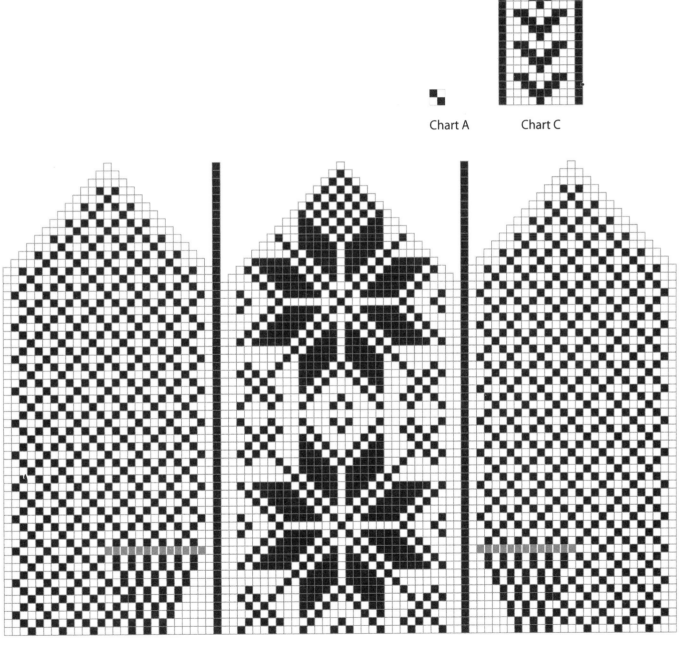

Chart A   Chart C

Chart B

𝒩HM #13

Source
Nordic Heritage Museum, Seattle, WA
Accession Number 2006.012.001

Finished Size
Girls Large or Women's Small
Length: 10.0" from cuff to fingertip
Width: 3.5" measured across palm

Yarn
Dalegarn Tiur (60% mohair 40% wool, 50g 115m)
MC: 0020 Natural, 1 skein
CC: 0090 Black, 1 skein

Gauge
32 sts and 30 rounds = 4"/10cm measured over palm

Needles & Notions
US Size 3 (3.00mm) DPN needles or size to give gauge
Waste Yarn, Tapestry Needle

THESE MITTENS ARE TEXTBOOK EXAMPLES OF THE MODERN SELBU MITTEN; A RIBBED CUFF SPORTS SYMMETRICAL STRIPES, THE CHECKERBOARD THUMB GUSSET, THE PATTERNED PALM AND LARGE STARS ON THE BACK ARE ALL TYPICAL FEATURES. THE ORIGINAL MITTENS WERE KNIT IN A DK-WEIGHT YARN BUT I HAVE CHOSEN A FINER DALEGARN TIUR TO FIT A MEDIUM LADIES HAND. KNIT IN JUMPER WEIGHT THEY WOULD FIT A CHILD. IF YOU WANT TO USE A PATTERNED CUFF INSTEAD OF RIBBING, CAST ON AROUND 54 STITCHES FOR YOUR CUFF, AND THEN INCREASE OR DECREASE A FEW STITCHES EVENLY AROUND TO WORK THE MAIN CHART. THE OLD MITTENS ARE WORKED WITH INCREASES A ROW OR TWO INTO THE MAIN PATTERN, SO DON'T FEEL LIKE YOU'VE MADE A MISTAKE IF YOU NEED TO DO THE SAME.

Cuff
Using MC, cast on 48 sts. Divide stitches evenly onto 4 needles and join circularly, taking care not to twist stitches. Work in K2P2 ribbing as follows:

8 Rounds MC
1 Round CC
1 Round MC
1 Round CC
2 Rounds MC
2 Rounds CC

2 Rounds MC
1 Round CC
1 Round MC
1 Round CC
4 Rounds MC.

Knit one Round in MC.

Lower Hand and Thumb Gusset
Begin Chart A, noting that charts are given for both Right and Left hands. Be sure to work one

palm and the back for each mitten; if the "other" palm gets distracting, try photocopying the page and folding over the side not in use. Work the lower hand and thumb gusset, increasing stitches as charted — 64 sts.

Set Aside Thumb

On the next Round, knit as charted until you reach the thumb, which is represented in the chart by the grey bar. Slip the 15 thumb stitches onto waste yarn and cast on 15 sts using a backward loop method. Work the rest of the chart, and finish the fingertip by cutting the yarn and threading it onto the tapestry needle. Then thread through the remaining stitches and pull tight.

Thumb

With palm up and fingertip facing you, pick up 15 sts from the stitches you cast on earlier. Pick up 1 st from side of thumb hole. Slip stitches from waste yarn onto needles. Pick up 1 st from side of thumb hole — 32 sts. Work thumb as charted, using Chart B for the outside of the thumb, and continuing the palm pattern for the inside of the thumb. Finish the thumb tip by cutting the yarn and threading it onto the tapestry needle. Then weave it through the remaining stitches and pull tight.

Finishing

Weave in ends on wrong side. If a small hole shows where the thumb was picked up, sew it closed using the yarn tail. Wash and block as desired.

Chart B

Chart A

Nhm #14

Source
Nordic Heritage Museum, Seattle, WA
Accession Number 86.008.013

Finished Size
Women's Small or Narrow Hands
Length: 10.0" from cuff to fingertip
Width: 3.5" measured across palm

Yarn
Jamieson's Spindrift (100% wool, 25g 105m)
MC: 304 Bleached White, 2 skeins
CC: 101 Shetland Black, 1 skein

Gauge
33 sts and 30 rounds = 4"/10cm measured over palm

Needles & Notions
US Size 2 (2.75mm) DPN needles or size to give gauge
Waste Yarn, Tapestry Needle

THESE ARE THE MITTENS THAT STARTED ME ON MY JOURNEY TO SELBU. LONG AND ELEGANT, THESE MITTENS STRUCK ME AT FIRST SIGHT WITH THEIR ELEGANT LACE CUFFS AND STARK PATTERNING. THE ORIGINAL MITTENS WERE NEVER WORN AND WERE STILL TIED TOGETHER AT THE TIPS. I HAVE TAKEN THE LIBERTY TO MODIFY THE CAST ON EDGE; THE ORIGINAL STARTED WITH A LONG-TAILED CAST-ON TURNED THE WRONG WAY WHICH LOOKED ROUGH AND SEEMED LESS STURDY THAN THE SMALL TURNED HEM I HAVE SUBSTITUTED IN ITS PLACE. KNIT THEM AS I HAVE IN CONTRASTING WHITE AND BLACK OR CHOOSE BRIGHTER COLORS FOR A WARMER EFFECT.

Stitch Patterns

Eyelet Cuff Lace (repeat of 11 sts)
Round 1: *ssk, k3, yo, k1, yo, k3, k2tog; repeat from * to end.
Round 2-4: knit all stitches.

Repeat these 4 rounds for pattern.

Cuff

Cast on 44 sts using long tailed method over two needles. Divide stitches evenly onto 4 needles. Join circularly, taking care not to twist stitches. Knit six rounds. Next Round, fold the hem to the inside (purl side) and pick up stitch through the stitch on the needle AND through the cast-on stitch rows below it. Pull new stitch through both to join the edge to the work.

Work Eyelet Cuff Lace as follows:

8 Rounds MC
2 Rounds CC
3 Rounds MC
1 Round CC
3 Rounds MC
1 Round CC
3 Rounds MC

2 Rounds CC
4 Rounds MC.

Knit 1 Round in MC, increasing every 5 sts 7 times — 51 sts.

Lower Hand

Begin Chart A, noting that charts are given for both Right and Left hands. Be sure to work one palm and the back for each mitten; if the "other" palm gets distracting, try photocopying the page and folding over the side not in use. Work the lower hand and thumb gusset, increasing 10 sts as charted — 61 sts.

Set Aside Thumb

On the next Round, knit as charted until you reach the thumb, which is represented in the chart by the grey bar. Slip the 15 thumb stitches onto waste yarn and cast on 15 sts using a backward loop method. Work the rest of the chart, and finish the fingertip by cutting the yarn and threading it onto the tapestry needle. Then thread through the remaining stitches and pull tight.

Thumb

Remove waste yarn and slip stitches all around the hole onto 4 needles, picking up one extra stitch between the front and back — 32 sts. Using MC and following Chart B for the front of the thumb, knit across thumb gusset stitches, slipping the two colored stitches that outline the thumb so that the stripe continues without interruption. Attach CC and work the palm-side of the thumb in pattern as established on the palm, decreasing over the stitches picked up from the side of the thumb hole — 30 sts. (This increase and then immediate decrease covers up the hole that invariably forms when adding the thumb.) Work Chart B. Finish the thumb tip by cutting the yarn and threading it onto the tapestry needle. Then weave it through the remaining stitches and pull tight.

Finishing

Weave in ends on wrong side. If a small hole shows where the thumb was picked up, sew it closed using the yarn tail. Wash and block as desired.

Original mittens
Nordic Heritage Museum, Seattle, WA
Accession Number 86.008.013

Chart B

Chart A

Nordic Heritage Museum

Seattle's Nordic Heritage Museum celebrates the contributions made by Nordic immigrants and their descendants, to the development of the Pacific Northwest. Exhibits and programming features each of the five Nordic countries: Norway, Sweden, Finland, Denmark, and Iceland.

The museum collection includes furniture and household items, papers, photos, and archival materials, and of course, a large collection of textiles. Knits, lace, embroidery, valuable weavings and rugs, and costumes and clothing, spinning wheels, looms, and much more.

In addition to historical programming, Nordic Heritage Museum has a wide range of activities and rotating exhibits of contemporary Nordic life: art exhibits, classes in traditional forms, Nordic movie nights, Young Nordics groups, musical programming, an annual Pippi Longstocking breakfast for kids, and more.

Running a museum is costly and labor intensive. Nordic Heritage Museum has established the Nordic Heritage Museum Endowment to provide ongoing financial support for the collection, storage, and maintenance of the museum collections. Your donations will allow the museum to continue caring for these precious resources, and keep them available for future research, as well as to continue providing cultural programs for the entire community. If you enjoy the patterns in this book, please consider making a tax-deductable donation to the museum at the address below.

Nordic Heritage Museum

3014 NW 67th St. NW
Seattle, WA 98117
(206) 789-5707

http://www.nordicmuseum.org/

Annemor Sundbø

In 1983, weaving instructor Annemor Sundbø purchased Torridal Tweed og Ulldynefabrikk, Norway's last remaining "shoddy," or wool recycling, factory. Torridal Tweed's huge piles of old, worn woolen garments to be shredded contained items dating from the beginning of the 20th century to the present; a treasure trove of Norway's every day knitting history.

Everyday Knitting - Treasures from a ragpile describes Annemor's journey through sixteen tons of rag pile. In tracing the use of the eight-pointed star motif she found the history of Norway's knitting traditions and the society that created them.

Everyday Knitting is lavishly illustrated with photos of the old knitted garments as well as diagrams, charts, and artwork showing knitting in history.

Early in my research process, my copy was on the coffee table when my parents-in-law came for a visit. Within a short time my engineer father-in-law had picked it up and become engrossed! It's fun to read as well as artistically inspiring.

Annemor's other titles include *Setesdal Sweaters: The History of the Norwegian Lice Pattern*, which tells the story of the famous luskofte sweater, and *Invisible Threads in Knitting,* an exploration of knitter's use of folk motifs and symbols and the magic they posses.

Bibliography

"About Us." Original Selbu. 12 Dec. 2006 http://www.selbuhusflid.no/.

Bondesen, Esther. *Den Nye Strikkeboken*. Oslo, Norway: Ansgar Forlag, 1947.

Bush, Nancy. *Folk Knitting in Estonia*. Loveland, CO: Interweave P, 1999.

Handmade in Selbu Norway. Selbu, Norway: Selbu Husflidscentral. (pamphlet)

"Info in English." Selbusjøen Hotell & Gjestegård. 12 Dec. 2006
    http://www.selbusjoenhotell.no/Default.asp?WCI=DisplayGroup&WCE=824&DGI=824

McGregor, Sheila. *Traditional Fair Isle Knitting*. New York: Dover Publications, 2003.

McGregor, Sheila. *Traditional Scandinavian Knitting*. Mineola, NY: Dover Publications,
    2004.

Odén, Birgitta. "Selbu Bygdemuseum Tekstkatalog." Ts. Trøndelag Folkemuseum,
    Trondheim, Norway. 2006.

Sibbern Bøhn, Annichen. *Norwegian Knitting Designs*. Oslo, Norway: Grondahl & Son,
    1965.

Sibberrn, Annichen. "Husflid of Industry." URD 29 Nov. 1930.

Starmore, Alice. *Fishermen's Sweaters - 20 Exclusive Knitwear Designs for All Generations*.
    North Pomfret, VT: Trafalgar Square Pub., 1993.

Starmore, Alice. *Scandinavian Knitwear 30 Original Designs From Traditional Patterns*. New
    York: Van Nostrand Reinhold Co., 1982.

"Strikkeutstilling." Selbu Bygdemuseum. Trøndelag Folkemuseum. 12 Dec. 2006
    http://www.selbu.kommune.no/skoler/Div/museum/.

Sundbø, Annemor. *Everyday Knitting: Treasures from a ragpile*. 2nd ed. Kristiansand,
    Norway: Torriedal Tweed, 2001.

Sundbø, Annemor. *Setesdal Sweaters*. Ose, Norway: Torriedal Tweed, 2001.

Til Strikkerne Av Selbuvotter. Selbu, Norway: Selbu Husflidscentral, 1934.

"Welcome to Selbu." Selbu Turistkontor. 12 Dec. 2006
    http://www.visitselbu.no/eng/index.html.

Zimmermann, Elizabeth. *Elizabeth Zimmermann's Knitter's Almanac Projects for Each Month
    of the Year*. Dover Ed. ed. New York: Dover Publications, 1981.

Last but not least...

Purists will say that your mittens must be knit in Norwegian yarn. I am not a purist. And besides, the traditional selbugarn yarn made for Selbu Husflid is no longer manufactured, so a substitution is inevitable. The samples in this book were knit with yarns that I thought would best duplicate the look-and-feel of the original, while also being generally available and attractive to knitters today. I love how "Esther's mittens" turned out; they were knit in a sport weight superwash I found at the bottom of my stash.

I recommend you choose a smooth yarn, in solid or lightly heathered colors. White with black, grey, or dark brown are very traditional but any colors that offer a good contrast can be (and were) used. A little fuzzy halo might be successful in designs with large blocks of pattern; for example, Dale Tiur. I have not received compensation by any yarn companies to use their yarn. Schoolhouse Press generously donated Jamieson & Smith and Satakieli when I asked. The other yarns were purchased online or at local yarn stores or supplied by the generous, talented knitters who made the samples. Here are a few vendors to get you started:

Schoolhouse Press
6899 Cary Bluff
Pittsville WI 54466

800-968-5648   info@schoolhousepress.com
http://www.schoolhousepress.com/
Jamieson & Smith, Satakieli

Dale of Norway Inc
4750 Shelbourne Road, Suite 2
Shelbourne, VT 05482

802 383 0132   mail@daleofnorway.com
http://www.dale.no/
Heilo, Baby Ull, Tiur, great yarns & prices

Arnhild's Knitting Studio
2315 Buchanan Drive
Ames, IA 50010

515-598-4391   arnhild@arnhild.com
http://www.arnhild.com/
Rauma yarns wholesale: see store listing

Two Swans Yarns
1-888-830-8269
http://www.twoswansyarns.com/
Fine yarns for traditional knitting

Hillesvåg Ullvarefabrikk AS
NO-5915 Hjelmås
NORWAY

56 35 78 00   hillesvaag@ull.no
http://www.ull.no/
HIFA yarns; email them for English

The Wooly West
P.O. Box 58306
Salt Lake City, UT 84158

888-487-9665   catalog@woolywest.com
http://www.woolywest.com/
Wide range of rare fine weight yarns